The Lighthearted Vegetarian Gourmet Cookbook

Steve Victor

Pacific Press Publishing Association
Boise, Idaho
Oshawa, Ontario, Canada

Acknowledgment and Dedication

I gratefully acknowledge the invaluable and indispensable assistance of Ruth Nelson, who helped to develop some of the recipes, cooked some of them, cleaned up after some of them, and ate all of them.

Ruth also assisted by her championship weightlifting, which provided further evidence to demolish the myths, that athletes, especially body builders and weight lifters, need extra protein or that a vegetarian diet is inadequate for anyone.

This book is dedicated to Ruth, and to all the millions of other people, growing in number every day, who have had the courage and fortitude to take one of the most difficult actions a human being can take—to go against twenty, forty, sixty, or more years of upbringing, conditioning, and societal and cultural influences, and change what they eat.

> Your greatest want is, you want much of meat.
> Why should you want? Behold the earth hath roots;
> Within this mile break forth a hundred springs;
> The oaks bear mast, the briers scarlet hips;
> The bounteous housewife nature on each bush
> Lays her full mess before you. Want? Why want?
> William Shakespeare
> *Timon of Athens,*
> act IV, scene III

Edited by Lincoln Steed
Designed by Tim Larson
Cover and inside illustrations by Kim McConnell
Type set in 10/11 Century Schoolbook

The author assumes full responsibility for the accuracy of all facts and quotations cited in this book.

Copyright © 1988 by
Pacific Press Publishing Association
Printed in United States of America
All Rights Reserved

Library of Congress Catalog Card Number: 87-62342

ISBN 0-8163-0718-0

91 92 · 5 4 3 2

Contents

Chapter 1: Why Was This Book Written?

(If you already know or don't care, go directly to chapter 2. Do Not Pass Go, Do Not Collect $200.)

I wrote this book because when I went looking for one like it, I couldn't find it.

Like many Americans, I had become convinced that cholesterol, fat, sugar, and salt were bad for my health, and therefore I sought to eliminate these from my diet. But when I went to the library and looked under "vegetarian" or browsed through bookstores at the latest in "health-food" cooking, most of the recipes I found contained large quantities of eggs, milk, cream, and cheese—rich sources of the very cholesterol and fats I was trying to avoid.

"True" vegetarianism is the complete avoidance of all animal products, whether from living, dead, or unborn animals, and the consumption only of vegetables. "Vegetable," as used in this context, is defined as "any plant that is eaten whole or in part," and therefore includes fruits, grains, and seeds.

Unfortunately, vegetarian cooking alone is not the answer to the cholesterol/fat problem. While cholesterol is found only in animal products, objectionably high levels of fats are found in some plant foods, as well. For example, soybeans are extremely fatty—over 50 percent of the calories in tofu (soy bean curd) come from fat! That is a greater percentage of fat than would be had in a completely trimmed T-bone steak.* While it is true that the beans contain unsaturated fat versus the saturated fat in the steak, my goal was to avoid any kind of fatty foods. This meant eliminating recipes which used not only soy products, but other fatty vegetarian foods such as oils (regardless of whether cold-pressed, hot-pressed, or "permanent-pressed"), avocados (88 percent fat), coconuts and coconut milk (92 percent fat), and the all-time favorite of health-food "nuts"—nuts. The ubiquitous nut, touted by backpackers in trail mix, by cereal companies in granola and granola bars, and by kiddie commercials (aimed at guilty super-moms) in peanut butter, runs about 70 to 80 percent fat, depending on the variety. The single exception is the chestnut, at about 7 percent fat. Water chestnuts are not true nuts and certainly do not mimic their namesakes in fat content.

Strictly speaking, sugar is a vegetable product, too, and you've certainly been lectured often enough on the evils of *that*, haven't you? (Come to think of it, honey, which is a common ingredient in virtually every "vegetarian" cookbook I looked through, is an animal product, isn't it?) Suffice it to say that these recipes contain no added sugar in any form, whether white,

---

*The source for this and all other food and nutrient analyses in this book, unless otherwise noted, is *Composition of Foods*, by Bernice K. Watt and Annabel L. Merrill, Tuscon, Arizona.

brown, or green; whether from cane, beet, bee, or fruit juice; whether as glucose, sucrose, fructose, dextrose, levulose, maltose, lactose, jocose, morose, or comatose.*

Salt is another issue. It is, as the game goes, not animal, or vegetable but mineral. Excess salt consumption is implicated in a number of health problems, most notably high blood pressure and stroke (although there is a considerable amount of evidence that high fat consumption is more important than high salt intake in contributing to these conditions). With one exception explained in the next paragraph, salt is not directly added in any of these recipes. I have never had a circulatory problem, though, so in just a few recipes (mostly Chinese) soy sauce is included where appropriate; use a low-sodium brand if you wish. If you eat no high-sodium foods otherwise and have one of these recipes once every two weeks or so (who wants to eat the same thing more often than that?), your total consumption of salt should still be well below the limits for most individuals. However, if you are currently on a low-sodium diet or have any type of circulatory or other health problem, either check with your doctor or omit these recipes. As an alternative to omitting these recipes, omit the soy sauce and increase the other herbs and spices.

The one exception to the salt rule is my recipe for "french fries." They're pretty good by themselves, but the addition of a tiny sprinkle of salt to the finished product seems to add that unique something. Again, on a once-a-month basis, this seems safe for healthy people; otherwise, try garlic or onion powder.

Now the answer to the question as to why I wrote this book should be more apparent. Very few recipes in any of the "vegetarian" or "health food" cookbooks I found, could meet these rather stringent standards, and those that did seemed for the most part rather insipid and bland. How many times can you eat steamed veggies over rice, whether at home or in a health-food restaurant? For that matter, what's left after you eliminate meat, fish, poultry, eggs, dairy products, oils, nuts, sugar, and salt? (This is a common reaction of nonvegetarians.) The answer, of course, is hundreds of vegetables, grains, fruits, herbs, and spices, which, with a little imagination, can be combined in thousands of combinations to produce a wide variety of delicious, satisfying, sensuous gourmet dishes.

I discovered this answer one step at a time. At first I took dishes from my old meat-eating days—such as, say, spaghetti and meat sauce—and found ways to make them using low-fat vegetable ingredients. Later, as I pored (mostly in vain) through "vegetarian" cookbooks, I would occasionally find a promising, tasty-sounding recipe which I could modify by removing the offending ingredients or substituting others to meet my standards. Eventually I became confident enough with my new repertoire of foods to start composing new dishes from scratch, and then refine them through experimentation.

Scrumptious Cuisine

The result has been the development of a new cuisine of scrumptious dinner menus. Contrary to the popular conception of vegetarian cooking as being dull (and sometimes well-deserved, in my opinion), my problem when I sit down to make up a list of menus for the week's shopping is not what to have, but which of many favorites to leave out. There are so many which are so good that I can't fit them all in a one- or two-week menu plan! And unlike most food designed for "diets," heart patients, or other sick people, or for consumption in health spas, the food's primary appeal is that it tastes great—and only incidentally is it healthful and—good news for the overweight—low-calorie.

Speaking of low-calorie, please note that these dishes were not created specifically for the purpose of weight loss, but without high-calorie items such as fats and sugars, they could hardly have come out otherwise. I have never been overweight, either by the medical tables or in my own thinking, but when I switched to this lifestyle (not "diet"—a diet is something you do temporarily, at the conclusion of which you go back to eating the way which made it necessary to diet in the first place), not particularly attempting to restrict my calorie intake and eating three or four times a day until I was satisfied, I lost over twenty previously unnoticed pounds of fat. The weight just melted off, over a period of six months to a year, without my going hungry, in fact, without my thinking about it or even noticing it for long intervals.

All of this, you may think, is a good reason to eat new dishes, but why write a book about it? Paradoxically, even though my original goal was not to lose weight but to obtain optimal health and longevity, it was probably the weight loss which, indirectly, was most responsible for inspiring this book. I do not engage in unsolicited proselytizing, of my diet or anything else, but the topic of food did come up often with friends and acquaintances, usually after they had noticed that I had lost weight and inquired how so. When I mentioned that I had become a vegetarian, many showed eager interest, for, despite all the current talk of health, longevity, and fitness, the primary motivator for most of us is still the mirror; and anything which offered the chance to shed unwanted pounds and be healthy (and full) at the same time (unlike most "crash" diets), was a prime topic for further discussion. Most people were initially wary of assumed gustatory blandness, but when I described my typical fare, eyes lighted up. Some asked for recipes, a few visited for dinner, one called with the unfortunate news that he had had a heart attack, knew I was into healthful living, and wondered whether I could offer any advice.

Told to Write

More and more suggested—yes, you guessed it—that I write a cookbook. They, too, had gotten interested in more healthful eating, had tried a few recipes in books or in the food section of the newspaper, and had found them wanting. But, not being chefs by vocation or avocation, they gave up, or floundered in the half-baked, half-deep-fried health advice so prevalent today. (Eat less red meat and more chicken and fish, says the newspaper article. But chicken and fish have about as much cholesterol as beef!) I, too, read the magazine and newspaper stories and realized that for the individual who is truly committed to making major dietary lifestyle changes to improve his/her health, but doesn't know what to eat or how to cook it, there is no place to learn, nowhere to turn.

So these recipes are humbly offered. If you are already following a health-oriented diet system, such as the Pritikin Program, the MacDougall Plan or Robert Haas' "Eat to Win," you should find that these recipes meet, and usually exceed, the standards of these programs. (Of course, this does not imply endorsement by any of these authors.) If you have been befuddled by advice to "cut down fat" and "reduce cholesterol" (usually followed by a recipe for chicken marinated in yogurt or snapper basted with olive oil) with no idea of how actually to achieve these goals, especially without discarding your taste buds, I hope this book will point you in a new direction.

I'm not quite sure what to call my new cuisine. Vegetarian actually isn't quite accurate, or at least insufficiently strict, for, as we have seen, vegetarian cooking can include dairy products, eggs, and fatty vegetable foods, which I omit. I could call it gourmet low-fat, low-sugar, low-salt vegetarian cooking, but that wouldn't have fit on the title page, would it?

Chapter 2: Introduction to the Recipes, Cooking Methods, and Ingredients. *Read This Chapter!*

How the Recipes Are Organized

Face it—ordinary American cooking is dull. Meat and potatoes, potatoes and meat, meat potatoes, potatoes meat. . . . The only variation, it seems, is which cut of meat and whether to roast, broil, or fry it. Oh, one or two nights a week, perhaps, meat from a dead pig or a dead sheep instead of a dead cow, and for the "health-conscious," an occasional dead chicken or dead fish. (Nothing about eating the *live* lobster, etc.!)

But look at the cornucopia of choice offered by the cuisines of much of the rest of the world! Faced with less affluence and/or less abundant meat supplies than Americans, many other cultures have developed imaginative ways of using their native grains and vegetables, seasoned with fragrant herbs and spices, to create a culinary range far beyond a piece of gray meat and a baked or fried potato. Even carnivores know the joy of an occasional foray to the local Italian, Chinese, or (perhaps, for the adventurous) Mexican restaurant, where beef, veal, chicken, and shrimp take on new flavors and aromas; such cuisines can provide a reassuringly familiar base for adventures with vegetarian dishes of the same genre. But how many people, of whatever dietary persuasion, are acquainted with the delights of, say, Indian or Middle Eastern cooking? Again, whether with or without meat, new joys await the diner who samples such fare.

Because ethnic cuisines, which do not rely on the flavor of plain meat as the centerpiece of a meal, provide such a variety of vegetarian dishes (far beyond the steamed-veggies-over-rice school), I have organized the recipes along ethnic lines, by country or region. These are predominately dinner dishes, so there is a section at the end of the book with lunch ideas and side dishes.

You may wonder why I have chosen to start with America. One reason is to provide something familiar for the xenophobic or for those whose experience with even ordinary Italian or Chinese restaurants is limited. The other reason is to show that even our much-maligned (and rightly so!) American staples can, in fact, be converted, with a little thought, from fast-food junk to healthful, nutritious, and tasty food.

Measures, Servings, and Analyses

Standard measures, as used in any cookbook, are employed throughout, with the exception of spices. Your tolerance for, say, garlic powder may be different from mine, (and your tolerance for cayenne pepper will almost certainly be *much* different from mine!) so I cannot tell you exactly how much to use. *De gustibus non disputandum est*— matters of taste cannot be debated—so in most cases I have given a suggested range, or used a term such as "pinch" or "generous," in which you can decide, based on your own experience with that particular ingredient, how much is "generous" for *you*. Where exact amounts are given, please consider them still only as suggested starting points, and feel free to vary according to your own palate. Make a note of how much you do use, though, so that if you later decide it was too bland or too spicy (or just right), you can adjust it, or repeat it, next time. Try starting in the middle, because while no one likes to take a bite and find too many tears streaming down his cheeks, chewing your way through a bland dinner is no fun, either. You might as well be at McBurger.

Servings are another personal matter. I don't know how many times (in my prevegetarian days) I've fixed a box of something that says, "serves six" and then later looked at the two empty plates and wondered what those other four people would have done for dinner if they'd been here. In my case, since I am very active in such sports as running and weight lifting, I find that I eat two or three times what the average cookbook author feels is a serving. On the other hand, if you are sedentary, trying to lose weight, older, very petite, or if you just prefer to nibble more frequent small meals rather than a few large ones, you may indeed eat less than the mythical "average" portion. Also please note that the sheer *quantity* of low-fat, high-fiber, low-calorie food required to make up a given 300-calorie serving is a lot greater than an equal-calorie serving of fatty food such as meat.

Therefore, what I have done with servings, in many cases, is given a range, such as "serves two to four." This means that, in my estimation, the dish prepared as described will serve as a satisfying dinner for two very hungry, physically active adults, three "average" appetites, or four moderate eaters. Make plenty—you don't want to run short, and almost everything in this book can be reheated for a delicious lunch or second, work-free dinner.

The nutrient analyses, fortunately, suffer from no such vagueness. The quantity analyzed is expressly stated, e.g. "one-fourth recipe," or "per cup," and then broken down by content of fat, protein, carbohydrate, calories, and percentage of calories from fat. Cholesterol content is not listed because, needless to say, it's zero in all dishes. (That was the whole idea, remember?)

The Russian Embassy's Favorite Friend: The Microwave

Microwave ovens are, in my opinion, the greatest thing to happen to vegetables since the invention of fire—and I'm not talking about just saving time, either. Because both fresh and frozen vegetables can be cooked quickly with no added water, flavor *and* nutrients are not leached out as they are in boiling, frying, etc. Corn on the cob can even be microwaved right in its husk, sealing in all the goodness and giving a burst of cornfield aroma when subsequently peeled and eaten. Other veggies are cooked in containers tightly sealed in plastic wrap, again preventing the escape of vitamins and flavors in drained water or steam.

Needless to say, the microwave oven is not suitable for every cooking task, but neither is any other appliance. You wouldn't attempt to bake a cake in your skillet or cook spaghetti in your oven, and there are foods which do not give best results in the microwave either. Yet the attempt by manufacturers of the same to promote their product as the jack-of-all-cooking—for example, by telling you to do your Thanksgiving turkey, Christmas roast, or breakfast eggs in the microwave—is probably responsible for most of the microwave disatisfaction around the country. I find that while potatoes can be baked reasonably well in a microwave if I am in an incredible hurry, they do not match a properly oven-baked spud for that crisp skin and flaky inside. Pastas are another example; they seem to fare better in a rolling boil of deep water than in the microwave.

Therefore, I have specified microwaving where I believe it to be the *best* method for taste and texture, so that the time and energy saved and easier cleanup are only added benefits. Generally, alternative cooking instructions are provided for those who do not have access to a microwave or who choose not to use them.

If you have a microwave and are concerned about its safety, have it checked for excess emissions by a factory-trained service technician or buy a testing device and check it yourself.

Water-Sautéing: Another Nail in the Coffin of OPEC (Organization of Producers of Extracts of Corn)

Sautéing in a skillet is just right where a crunchy texture is desired or a bit of browning (both weak points of the microwave) or for various other reasons. And it *can* be done without oil or butter in the pan. Use much lower heat, a nonstick skillet (an electric skillet, set to about 240-260 degrees is about ideal), and stir frequently to prevent sticking. Use only a little bit of water at first—perhaps a couple of tablespoons, then, as the water boils off, add more as needed to prevent sticking. (Some extremely watery vegetables, such as onions, can be done with no water at all if the heat is very low.) Why not simply add enough water at first to take care of all that, you ask? Because then the result is closer to braising or boiling.

The first time you use water in your pan instead of oil you may miss that burned-fat, burned carbohydrate taste which we have been brought up to think is good. I did, on my first batch of Chinese stir-fry. But on my second batch, I noticed that I could taste the flavors of the vegetables themselves instead of the flavor of grease and wouldn't go back now even if I didn't care about all the dire health consequences of fat.

In a few cases where adding water is not feasible or desirable, I have suggested instead the use of a nonstick vegetable coating spray. It accomplishes the objective with only a very small amount of actual fatty ingredient, and the amount absorbed into the food is even smaller. In sautéing, of course, leave the pan uncovered, unless otherwise specified, so that, as mentioned above, the water can evaporate and allow some browning to occur. Where covered cooking is specified, you may be surprised at how much water gathers in the bottom of the pan, demonstrating the high water content of most vegetables and eliminating the need for adding additional liquid. Usually this is done where it is desirable to accumulate a broth, but if it gets too watery, uncover briefly as needed. Also, be sure to add only *hot* tap water, not cold, so you don't slow down the cooking and cause sogginess.

It's in the Can

One of the side effects of the growing health/diet consciousness in America is that an increasing number of canned goods can now be found in no-salt-added versions. Especially common are no-salt tomatoes, tomato puree, and tomato paste. Other canned items are much harder to find in salt-free versions. In fact, with beans such as kidney or pinto beans, I have to hunt assiduously to find cans without *sugar,* and occasionally oil, and most of these come with several added preservatives as well, usually calcium chloride and calcium disodium EDTA (rattled those off pretty impressively, huh?). I finally located one store which carries pinto beans packed only in water and salt, and another which does the same for black and pink beans, and a third for kidney beans. To minimize trips, when I go to any of these stores I buy a dozen cans of the particular product, and that lasts a while. I still drain them thoroughly, and you could go so far as to rinse them too, though you might lose a little flavor.

What if you are on a strictly limited-salt diet? Then you have the option of doing the canner's work yourself by preparing dried beans from scratch, usually by soaking them overnight and simmering them, or perhaps by the quicker method of boiling without soaking (there are directions printed on each package of dried beans). However, it is a matter for each individual to consider convenience versus dietary needs (unless, of course, the decision has been made for you, either by your doctor or by a condition such as high blood pressure). What I have done in the recipes, therefore, is to list an ingredient such as "2 cups cooked pinto beans." This means either that amount of canned beans, *thoroughly drained,* or enough dried beans reconstituted and cooked to make two cups.

What if you can't find salt-free tomato products or the other few canned goods called for? Start hounding your store manager to carry them. Check other stores, too, as I did for sugar- and oil-free beans, and let him know you're going to do so!

11

Chapter 3: American: Be It Ever So Humble

As promised, our trip around the world starts right here at home. And what could be more comforting than to start with that quintessential favorite,

The All-American Shamburger

Ah, the hamburger! Whether frozen and thawed in a fast-food joint, or piled with bacon, cheese, avocado, and any other 90 percent-fat ingredients they can think of in a nouveau/yuppie steak house, Americans can't get enough of hamburgers. With condiments and garnishes, truly a meal on a bun—such as it is.

Most vegetarian cookbooks have one or more recipes for meatless hamburgers, invariably involving soybeans, or perhaps nuts, thereby attempting to duplicate the taste of the burger by duplicating its fattiness. Many also use oil or call for frying in oil. All of this, of course, only confirms that the original burger itself didn't have much taste besides that of grease; it was the toppings that gave it some taste. (Does anyone ever order a burger absolutely plain—no ketchup, pickles, onions, *nothing?*)

Our recipe, on the other hand, uses no fatty ingredients or oils. It's low in calories, high in nutrition and taste, and so versatile—in later chapters it will be a basis for meatballs and for sausage submarines. In fact, it could be used just about anywhere a meat patty is called for. Use your imagination.

Buns Are Important

You certainly don't want to use ordinary store-bought ones, made with white flour, sugar, shortening, and possibly eggs. Fortunately, a wide variety of alternatives are available at a good natural-foods store. READ THE LABELS. You want those made with only whole wheat, not a mixture of white and whole-wheat flour, and without eggs. Some will have honey or molasses to feed the yeast—remember that ingredients are listed in descending order of predominance, and the lower these are listed, the better. Watch out for oils—usually "cold-pressed safflower oil." The same thing applies, if you can't find any with no shortenings. A few use lecithin, hoping you won't recognize it as a fat. An easy way to check the level of fat, without doing a lot of fancy math, is to look at the nutrient table on the package (don't buy it if it doesn't have one) and see how many grams of fat there are per bun. One gram is excellent, two is good, three is forget it. If they take the sneaky way out by using a serving measure other than one bun (such as, say, per ounce), look at the number of calories per whatever their serving size is. There should be no more than one gram of fat for each 70-100 calories per serving, which, again, is two grams per typical 120-160 calorie bun.

Here's the burger recipe, along with some accompaniments—sugar free ketchup and, believe it or not, french fries.

13

Shamburgers

2 lbs. eggplant (2 medium to large),
    peeled and chopped fine or
    grated in a food processor
2-5 cloves garlic, crushed
1 large onion, minced
1 c. yellow cornmeal
1 c. old-fashioned (not quick cooking)
    rolled oats
2 c. Shredded Wheat cereal, crushed
    or ground in a blender to yield
    about one cup
Garlic powder
Onion powder

Place eggplant, garlic, and onion in non-stick skillet, cover, and cook about 10 minutes over low to moderate heat. Stir occasionally, adding a little water if needed to prevent sticking, until eggplant is tender.

While eggplant cooks, combine cornmeal, oats, wheat cereal in a large mixing bowl. Add cooked mixture and mix thoroughly. Allow to cool. When cool enough to work with comfortably, form eight patties. If any will not be used at this time, wrap tightly in plastic wrap and refrigerate, for up to several days. Season others with pepper, garlic and onion powder to taste on both sides.

To cook one or two at a time, spray non-stick skillet with nonstick vegetable coating. Fry over medium heat, covered, until one side is browned and a bit crisp. Turn and brown other side, covered; then reduce heat and continue to cook covered, turning again if necessary, for total of about 20 minutes.

To cook more at once, spray broiling pan with nonstick coating, broil patties on second-highest oven rack for 5-10 minutes per side, until brown on both sides.

To warm buns, split and place face down on top of patties in covered fry pan. For toasted buns, place under broiler or place face down directly on surface of skillet while burgers cook.

Yield: 8 burgers. Depending on size of bun and accompaniments, most adults will eat two, but moderate eaters may want only one.

PER BURGER:

Protein 5g
Carbohydrates............................. 40g
Fat...1.5g
Calories...188
Fat by Calories 7%

Note: Add nutrients from buns from analysis on bun package.

Serving suggestions: Place on warmed or toasted split buns (see above) and garnish with lettuce, tomato, thickly sliced red (Bermuda) onion, homemade ketchup (see below).

Ketchup

Commercial ketchups can derive over 50 percent of their calories from sugar! Here's the easy way to make sugar-free ketchup at home:

4 oz. tomato purée
2-8 tablespoons vinegar
Garlic powder
Onion powder

Combine all ingredients in small bowl, seasoning to taste. Mix thoroughly. Excess may be refrigerated, tightly covered, for a few days. May require a little additional vinegar or water after being refrigerated.

Nutrients: About 5 calories per tablespoon, virtually all from carbohydrate.

Healthful French Fries

Hamburger and fries! It's practically one word—burgeranfries. Most people wouldn't think of eating one without the other. Yet I find this recipe so satisfying and tasty that rather than eat a relatively small amount as a side dish with the shamburgers, I'd rather make a whole slew and have them as a main course for dinner, with a tossed salad on the side. Not only is that a delicious, filling meal, it's also ultra-low-calorie—wait until you see the nutrient table. For, as almost everyone knows by now, potatoes aren't fattening (in fact, they're one of the lowest-fat foods around—much lower in fat than lettuce, on a percent-of-calories basis); it's what you put on them, or do to them, which makes them fattening (just like pasta, as we'll see).

Yes, in the old days, they used to torture people by boiling them in oil. Now we torture our potatoes—and our waistlines—by boiling them (our potatoes, not our waistlines) in oil, thereby *tripling* the calorie count! If numbers mean nothing to you, think of it this way: You could eat three times as many of my French fries as of conventional greasetrap fries, for the same calorie "cost."

So how do you get a crunchy potato without hot oil? As the term *air-fried* implies, you use hot air—*very* hot. Slice them thickly so that the outside will get brown and crisp by the time the inside is done.

Flavor note: These fries are good plain, or with one or more seasonings such as garlic powder, onion powder, paprika, or cayenne pepper. However, this is to me the one recipe out of everything I eat in which the addition of pure salt seems to be worth it in terms of taste. And why should it not be so? Our problem in America is not that we salt one or two foods, it's that we salt everything, either in processing, in cooking, or at the table. We turn our culinary noses up at people who put ketchup on everything, and you wouldn't sprinkle cayenne pepper on everything you ate (would you?), yet both have their place in certain dishes. Try the fries yourself, with various seasonings, and if you don't have a salt problem, see what you think about it, with and without.

*P.S. If you want to put my homemade ketchup (page 14) on your fries, please feel free to do so, but please don't tell me about it.

French Fry Recipe
About 4 lb. large baking potatoes, scrubbed but *not* peeled.

Preheat oven to 475˚. Spray two baking sheets (preferably nonstick) with nonstick vegetable spray. Cut half the potatoes into discs about a quarter inch thick. Cut the rest in half lengthwise, and then at angles longitudinally to made wedge-shaped "steak fries." Place discs on lower baking sheet in oven and steak fries on upper sheet, using lower-middle and upper-middle oven positions, respectively. When discs are brown on one side (about 15-25 minutes) turn and continue baking until brown on both sides. Some will "souffle" (puff up) beautifully, an effect which is tricky to achieve for French chefs using oil! When discs are done, serve them and lower heat to 350˚. By the time you are through eating the discs, the wedges, which have not had the hot metal against

their sides and rely only on the hot air to brown, will be done and ready to serve. Season as above.

Note: These lose something in reheating, so make only what you need—which will probably be more than you think the first time!

Yield: As a side dish, allow one pound per person; as a main dish, two or more pounds of raw potatoes per person. (A very small potato is about four ounces; a medium one is about eight; a large one is about twelve.)

PER RAW POUND

Protein	9g
Carbohydrates	77g
Fat	0.5g
Calories	345
Fat by Calories	1%(!)

Other Ways to Do Your Spuds

Man does not live by French fries alone—although kids do. When you don't want to do all that slicing, or want a different taste (and for those recipes calling for them), here are other ways to cook potatoes.

To bake: Place cleaned potatoes in middle of preheated 450˚ oven. After 30 minutes, pierce both sides with a fork twice and replace in oven, with opposite side up. They will be done in another 20-40 minutes, depending on size; test by piercing deeply with fork or thin knife to see if tender. Try seasoning with chives as well as black pepper.

To boil: Do not peel potatoes. Smaller varieties such as red or white are especially suitable. Cut into large chunks and place in boiling water. Simmer, covered, about 25-35 minutes, until tender to fork or knife. Drain and season with parsley.

To mash: Prepare unpeeled, boiled potatoes and mash with ricer, masher, flower pot, whatever, adding a little hot water if needed to achieve desired consistency. Mash in parsley, black and white pepper, and (optional) garlic or onion powder.

Nutritional note: The nutrient composition of the variously cooked potatoes does not change significantly, on a percentage basis.

Enough of this ersatz meat and potatoes! Let's start our global circumnavigation with a trip to our neighbors south of the border.

Chapter 4: Mexican: Ole!

In Los Angeles, where I live, taco stands now seem to outnumber hamburger stands—and, for that matter, most of the hamburger stands, other than the national chains, offer tacos as well. Mexican cooking, of a somewhat nouvelle variety, has also made its way into the trendy, upscale eateries—there are Mexican restaurants in which dinner for two can reach $60, not counting, as they say, tax, tip, or beverage. (I personally favor a no-atmosphere joint on the east side in which two of us have stuffed ourselves silly for one-tenth that amount.)

The rest of the country, which is minus the proximity and the large Mexican population of the City of the Angels, has probably not "progressed" quite so far in its appreciation of *las comidas Mexicanas*. Nevertheless, its popularity is growing everywhere, for the same reasons—good, tasty food at (usually) very reasonable prices, offering something different from the usual fare, but with familiar American staples, such as ground beef or chicken, for the cautious.

The nonmeat staples of Mexican cooking, such as tortillas, beans, rice, chili peppers, and tomatoes, offer bounteous fare for the vegetarian, especially when flavored with spices such as cumin and cayenne. Some of my first experiments in vegetarian cooking were in the Mexican genre, because I was already familiar with dishes such as burritos and tostadas, and because it was easy to substitute rice and beans for a filling in place of meat. (In fact, you can do it in a Mexican restaurant, and so enjoy a vegetarian meal even when out with carnivorous friends.)

Don't stereotype all Mexican cooking as "hot." Although I feel that Mexican dishes are prime evidence against the vegetarian-is-bland-and-boring school of thought, you may make these dinners as mild as you like; if you start mild, you may (or may not) find that you gradually build not only an increasing tolerance but also a taste for some of the more pungent spices. Everything said earlier about spicing is especially applicable here. If you do not wish to use the sharp cayenne pepper which is listed in a number of the recipes, you may substitute a finely minced fresh green chile (for a very mild flavor), a finely minced fresh jalapeño (for a stronger flavor), or increase the amount of cooked jalapeño peppers called for in the recipe (for a spice that will equal that of the cayenne, but of a slightly different "feel").

About Millet

"Millet" is not the answer to the riddle "What do you do to grain?" It *is* a grain. Long a staple in parts of Russia, Eastern Europe, and Asia, it is sold in this country primarily as a part of hamster food or bird seed. Since very few birds die of heart disease, that's their gain and our loss. Millet, which is available at almost any health-food store, is an extremely bland grain which, while contributing little flavor of its own, has a remarkable ability to absorb the flavors of other ingredients, and therefore makes an excellent base or filler. This chameleonlike versatility allows it to appear in dishes of many different types and cuisine styles.

17

While it is not, strictly speaking, a part of traditional Mexican cooking, I first used it in burritos, mostly because I was getting tired of eating all the rice which was a component of almost every "vegetarian" dish I had tried. Serendipity of serendipities, its mildness perfectly complemented the spiciness of the rest of the recipe, while the tiny grains lent texture to the smooth bean paste. It wasn't long before I was using it in other recipes where these qualities seemed appropriate.

Along with all the other nutritional virtues of whole grains, millet is extremely high in iron (see Postscript); combined with the high iron content of beans, it's surprising nails don't sprout out of the burrito filling. A final virtue is ease of preparation: add three parts water (hot tap water will boil faster than cold, but it doesn't matter to the recipe) to one part millet, bring to boil, stir, cover tightly, and reduce heat to low. (If your pot lid is really tight, you can shut the heat off completely.) Allow to steam 20-30 minutes, depending on quantity, until millet is tender and all water is absorbed. It's now ready to serve or to use in recipes.

Because millet has no gluten, it is ideal for those who are allergic to wheat. If for any reason you prefer not to use it, or simply wish an occasional change, you may substitute an equal quantity of brown rice in virtually any recipe.

About Tortillas

Tortillas are available in most supermarkets these days, often in several varieties. You want corn tortillas—flour tortillas are made with lard or shortening and refined (white) flour. Occasionally you may find whole wheat tortillas; these are a pleasant change of pace, but check the label carefully for added fats. Even among corn tortillas, considerable label-reading is necessary. The best will simply read "Stone ground corn, water, lime." Other brands may treat the corn with methoxycellulose, or add dough conditioners and preservatives (without which the Mexicans have done very handily for centuries, thank you). Still others may use corn flour, which suffers fiber loss from being more highly refined. If you can't find what you want at the supermarket, try your friendly natural-food store again (and, of course, gripe to the manager!).

Burritos

Filling:
1/2 c. raw millet
2 c. cooked pinto beans (drain thoroughly if canned)
1 or more jalapeño peppers
3 fresh green chilies, mild type
Garlic powder
Onion powder
Paprika
Cumin
Cayenne pepper
Oregano
Lettuce, shredded
Tomato, chopped, about one large or two medium
Onion, chopped, one medium-large
One package of 12 corn tortillas
One 7 1/2 oz. or 10 1/2 oz. can tomatoes and green chilies, divided

Preheat oven to 350°. Cook millet with 1 1/2 cups water, as per directions above. Rinse jalapeños and chilies and place on a small sheet of aluminum foil (for easy cleaning) or on a baking sheet in center of oven. While millet and peppers cook, mash beans with potato masher in mixing bowl. Add spices to taste—a generous sprinkling of all except cayenne, of which just a pinch. Pour about 4-5 ounces of the canned tomatoes and chilies into a small bowl for the sauce; add remainder to bean mix. Check peppers for doneness and turn if necessary; they are done when skin has lost its shininess and begun to wrinkle. (Outer skin may start to peel away, and some browning will occur; do not let them get too brown or soft.) When peppers are done, remove from oven and allow chilies to cool, to be used as a garnish.

Chop jalapeño very fine. Add about a quarter of chopped jalapeño to bean mix; reserve rest for sauce. (Note: this recipe makes a somewhat spicy filling and a very spicy sauce. For milder palates, omit jalapeño entirely or, if "some like it hot" and some don't, have the wimpier eaters not use the sauce.) Stir bean mixture thoroughly.

When millet is done, add bean mixture to millet and stir. Continue heating mixture over low heat, covered, stirring occasionally, while preparing tortillas (and sauce, if not done yet).

Sauce:

Combine remaining canned tomatoes and chilies and jalapeño peppers. Add same spices as above; see note on spicing. Stir well and heat, covered, in small saucepan or in microwave oven, very gently until heated through. Do not boil or "cook" sauce.

Tortillas:

Bring 1" of water to boil in large skillet (an electric skillet is ideal). Place tortillas, one or two at a time, on rack above water. Cover very tightly and reduce heat so water just barely bubbles. Steam for about a minute or until tortillas are soft; do not overcook. Serve immediately.

For mass preparation: Place stack of tortillas in aluminum foil, and a few drops of water, wrap tightly, and bake in 350° oven about 15 minutes. Keep remaining servings warm by rewrapping foil tightly after removing each serving; turn off oven heat.

To microwave: Place each tortilla between two dampened paper towels and microwave on high power, one or two at a time, about 60 seconds or until soft and warm. Be careful not to overcook. Serve immediately.

To serve burritos: Place warmed tortilla flat on plate. Cut tops from green chilies and slice into strips, removing ribs and seeds. Lay a chili strip across tortilla just below the middle. Spread a few tablespoons of filling on chili, also in strip-style. Spoon 1/2 to 1 tablespoon of warmed sauce over filling. Sprinkle chopped onion, tomato, and lettuce over filling. Fold tortilla up from bottom, wrap in sides if you have any room (I usually don't), and roll up to top. (It probably won't stay together very well unless you have jumbo tortillas. So what?) Pick up and eat out of hand for a messy but very tasty meal.

Variations: Substitute 1/2 cup uncooked brown rice, cooked to yield about 1 1/2 cups (or 1 1/2 cups leftover rice—an ideal way to use leftovers), for millet, or substitute about 1 1/2 cups coarsely mashed potatoes (again, an ideal leftover usage) for millet. Nutritional data will change only minimally.

Yield: 3-6 burritos per person (fewer if you have side dishes), serves 2-4.

PER BURRITO

Protein 5g
Carbohydrates 26g

Fat...1.5g
Calories 130
Fat by Calories 10%

Note: Based on average tortilla of about 60 calories; may vary depending on tortilla purchased.

You may have wondered if you could ever enjoy Mexican food without the ubiquitous glop of melted cheese covering everything. Once you taste other flavors, such as the beans, chilies, and spices, which were formerly overwhelmed by the tastes of fat and salt blanketing your food, you'll find it preferable—as you'll also see when we come to Italian food.

For a change in texture, appearance, and taste, here are a couple of variations on the same theme. The first one adds "crunch," which some people thought would not be possible without the use of oil-frying.

Tostadas

Prepare burrito filling and sauce, as outlined above, but do not steam tortillas. Instead, spread them out on two baking sheets and bake in 350° oven about 15 minutes or until crisp and light brown, turning halfway through. Spread filling, sauce, and garnishes over whole surface and eat as an open-faced sandwich. Watch out—they tend to break if you don't bite carefully!

Snack note: Preparing the tortillas this way makes an ideal snack or side dish all by itself—more corn taste and crunch than commercial taco chips or corn chips, without the oil and salt.

Taco Casserole

Prepare Burrito Filling, but do not make a separate sauce—instead, use all of the canned tomatoes and green chili in the filling. Meantime, bake tortillas as for tostadas, above. When both are done, pour filling into 9-10" glass casserole dish, break up tortillas into bite-sized chips, and mix into filling. Smooth top and spread green chili strips on surface. Microwave on about 2/3 power ("Bake" or "Roast") for 3-8 minutes until thoroughly heated. Top with chopped lettuce and tomato spread generously over entire surface. Serve immediately, or, for a taste change, cook 1-3 minutes more or until toppings are heated through but not cooked. For conventional oven, bake filling without corn chips about 10 minutes, covered, then mix in corn chips and bake another 5 minutes, covered. Proceed as above for toppings, with same options.

Note: Do not overcook, or corn chips will get too soggy. For even crisper chips, do not add corn chips until last 1-3 minutes of cooking, whether in microwave or conventional oven.

Yield and nutritional data are same as burritos, minus insignificant change from lack of onions.

For additional variations, fill whole-wheat pitas with burrito filling and garnishes (this is a bit neater and easier to carry for lunch, if you have a microwave at work to reheat them), or use filling as a dip for the corn chips. Use your imagination!

Potatoes With Bean Dip

If you scoffed at my earlier suggestion that baked potatoes could be enjoyed without sour cream or butter, wait until you try these! They're a great main dish with just a tossed salad on the side.

4 large baking potatoes, or 3 lb. of smaller ones
2 c. cooked pinto beans (one 16-oz. can, drained)
Garlic powder
Onion powder
Cayenne
Paprika
Cumin
Green chilies (optional)
Water

Bake potatoes as per instructions on page 15. Mash beans in bowl, adding a little water as needed for a smooth, diplike consistency. Add spices to taste. Microwave or heat in small saucepan on moderate heat setting, stirring occasionally and thinning with water if needed. If using chilies, roast carefully while potatoes bake, allowing less time due to higher heat setting of oven. Cut off tops and cut into strips, removing ribs and seeds.

To serve: Split baked potatoes in half lengthwise. Fluff up meat slightly with fork. Spread dip over each half and top with a green chili strip, if desired. May easily be reheated in microwave if there are any leftovers, but heat dip and potatoes separately.
Yield: Serves 2 (most likely) to 4.

PER 12 OZ. POTATO WITH 1/4 OF DIP RECIPE

Protein	13g
Carbohydrates	76g
Fat	0.8g
Calories	436
Fat by Calories	1.7%(!)

Chili

This is the archetypal Mexican dish, one which Texans also seem to want to claim as their own. Both versions, of course, are based on meat, with die-hard purists aghast at any dilution of same by beans or even onions. Yet the name of the dish refers simply to any preparation stewed with chili peppers; the full name of the meat dish is *chili con carne,* literally "chili with meat." Obviously, then, if the "con carne" is not there, you have a perfectly legitimate preparation without meat. We will call it, in Spanish, *chili sin carne* (chili without meat).

Needless to say, all comments made in the section on burritos regarding spicing apply here, also. Make your chili as hot or as mild as you like. (By the way, I could never figure out why I bought chili powder for so many years, once I read the ingredients: cayenne, cumin, garlic, and perhaps onion or paprika. Why not add them separately yourself, in your own desired proportions, instead of paying someone a good deal of money to mix them for you and sell it as one package?)

Chili Sin Carne
2-6 cloves garlic, peeled and crushed
2 large onions, cut into long strips
1 green bell pepper, cored, seeded, and de-ribbed, chopped finely
1 large (28-30 oz.) can tomato puree
1 large or 2 16-oz. cans tomatoes, with juice
1 large or 2 16-oz. cans kidney or pink beans, or 4 cups beans cooked from scratch
3 fresh mild green chilies (substitute one, two, or all three with yellow, red, serrano, or other hotter peppers for a hotter dish)

Garlic powder
Onion powder
Paprika
Cumin
Cayenne

Sauté garlic, onions, and bell pepper in a little water in 5-6 quart saucepan until almost tender. For a little extra flavor, allow onions to brown slightly. Add tomato puree and juice from canned tomatoes. Cut tomatoes into chunks and add to pot. Drain beans and add. Add whole chilies and spices to taste, being very generous with all except cayenne. Bring just to boil, reduce heat, cover, and simmer, stirring occasionally, for at least 1 hour, making sure whole chilies are tender, and preferably for several hours or all day. (To me this chili always seems to taste even better as leftovers. So you may make it up to several days in advance, cool, refrigerate, and reheat on serving day.)

To serve: My favorite accompaniment to chili is hot cooked brown rice. Place 1 to 1 1/2 cups rice in bowl, ladle chili on top, and as you come to the large green chilies, cut the tops off and cut in chunks—say, halves or thirds—and top each person's serving with a chunk of green chili.

Alternate serving suggestions: Instead of rice, serve chili with or over cornbread (page 78) or by itself with hot whole-wheat tortillas on the side. Sloosh the tortilla through the chili before each bite of tortilla for proper effect.

For all serving variations, a tossed salad (page 73) is ideal.

Yield: By itself (not recommended!) serves 2-4. With rice, cornbread, or tortillas, serves 4-8, depending not only on appetite but also on ratio of chili to accompaniment. Figure 1/8 recipe plus 1 to 1 1/2 cups rice for small dinner serving; 1/4 recipe plus 2 to 3 cups rice for very large dinner serving.

PER 1/4 RECIPE

Protein 20g
Carbohydrates 74g
Fat 1.8g
Calories 368
Fat by Calories 4.5%

Note: Add figures for appropriate amount of desired accompaniment—see rice chart on page 27 or chart on tortilla package.

Mexican Stuffed Peppers

Tired of frozen stuffed peppers, filled with the inevitable beef and rice mixture? These peppers are not only vegetarian, but they use corn as the main starch, rather than millet or rice, as the other recipes have so far.

**4 very large or more smaller green
   bell peppers**
1 medium onion, chopped
2-3 cloves garlic, crushed
2 16-oz. cans tomatoes
1/2 c. cornmeal
1/4 to 1 tsp. cayenne pepper
1/2 tsp. cumin
1/2 tsp. paprika
**1 c. frozen or canned corn, drained
   (about 2/3 of a 10-oz. package of
   frozen)**
**1 c. (1/2 can) cooked pinto, pink, or kid-
   ney beans, drained**

Water-sauté onion and garlic in 2-quart saucepan until tender. Add juice from tomatoes. Chop and add tomatoes. Add cornmeal and spices. Stir and cook, covered, over moderate heat about 15 minutes, stirring occasionally, until mixture thickens, then add corn and beans and continue to heat over low heat until thoroughly hot.

While mixture cooks, cut top off each pepper and save. Remove seeds and ribs. Place peppers upright in deep glass or ceramic casserole dish. Fill each pepper with stuffing mixture and replace tops on peppers. If you have room, fill a heat-proof glass measuring cup half full with water and place in center of casserole; otherwise, put about 1/2" hot water in casserole. Save any leftover stuffing. Microwave casserole covered on about 60 percent power ("Bake") for 30 minutes, rotating each pepper and the entire dish halfway through, or bake at 350° 30-45 minutes or until peppers are tender but not mushy.

To serve: A few minutes before peppers are done, reheat any leftover stuffing. When done, place peppers on plates, split in half vertically, and spoon extra stuffing, if any, over split halves.

Yield: In my hungrier moments, I have been known to eat the entire thing myself. Normally, serves two: could be stretched to serve more with an accompaniment such as cornbread.

PER PEPPER

Protein	11g
Carbohydrates	55g
Fat	1.4g
Calories	257
Fat by Calories	5%

Sloppy Joes

This traditional barbecue dish may be considered more American than Mexican; I have included it here because of the similarity of ingredients to some of the other Mexican dishes. The barbecue sauce is the distinguishing feature. If you want a dish more similar to our American entrees, cook Shamburgers (page 14), but after broiling or frying, break up burger on buns and pour over a barbecue sauce made as in the recipe below.

Commercial barbecue sauce, of course, suffers from the same sugar-richness as its brother, commercial ketchup. The various additives designed to give it smoke flavor only make it worse. The sharp-eyed may note that the bit of apple-juice concentrate in this recipe is an exception to an earlier statement concerning added sweeteners; purists may choose to omit it or substitute either a sweet spice, such as oregano or basil, or some minced green or red bell pepper (red ones are especially sweet).

1 1/2 c. cooked brown rice (1/2 c. raw)
2 c. cooked pinto beans
2 medium onions, chopped
1 6-oz. can tomato paste
Water
Vinegar
Garlic powder
Onion powder
1 to 2 tbsp. frozen apple juice concentrate, thawed
4 hamburger buns (see page 13)

Sauté onions in water in skillet or saucepan until tender, allowing to brown slightly. Add rice and beans. Add tomato paste and 1 can water. Add 1/2 to 1 can vinegar, spices, and juice. Stir and taste; add either water or vinegar, or both, as mixture cooks, to adjust both sauce consistency and sharpness. Continue to simmer covered, adjusting spices as needed, until thoroughly heated. When almost done, split hamburger buns and toast under broiler to desired crispness.

To serve: Place toasted bun halves open-face style on plate and cover with hot mix. Do *not* attempt to eat with hands!—use knife and fork. Serve a tossed salad on the side.

Yield: 4 buns (8 halves) serves 2-4

PER 1/4 RECIPE

Protein	10g
Carbohydrates	49g
Fat	1g
Calories	240
Fat by calories	4%

Note: Add values for hamburger buns chosen.

Variation: Add a pinch of crushed red pepper flakes to mix for a spicy barbecue sauce.

The magic carpet of cookery now whisks us across the Pacific, instantly!

Chapter 5: Chinese

(A Day After You Have It, You'll Want It Again)

Chinese cooking is currently undergoing quite a boom in America, among both gourmets and the health-conscious (and health-conscious gourmets). Aside from the fact that vegetarian dishes appear on most Chinese restaurant menus, the method of preparation is often very close to our own, using just one or two tablespoons of oil in a hot wok to stir-fry vegetables and small pieces of meat or seafood. Unfortunately, many restaurants still go fairly heavy on the soy sauce and sugar (some sweet-and-sour dishes or sauces are almost candylike), but more and more are omitting the formerly universal monosodium glutamate, or will do so on request, and a number will skip the sugar and salty stuff on request too.

Chinese restaurants, therefore, can be a haven for the health-conscious traveler (I always seek them out when I'm in a strange city) or gourmet who enjoys eating out, but you are still stuck with refined, fiber-deficient white rice (and remember to stay away from the bean curd, or tofu, also—see page 5. Care must be exercised, too, in watching out that eggs don't sneak in, in such dishes as egg drop soup or mu shu. Since the latter is generally prepared fresh to order, you can ask to have the eggs omitted; one particularly clever restaurant near me, which advertises a low-cholesterol menu, used only egg whites in its mu shu, since virtually all of the cholesterol is in the yolk.

Alas, China's neighbors in Southeast Asia do not offer much hope for the healthy in their cuisine. Vietnamese, Thai, Indonesian, and Cambodian restaurants generally use much more oil in cooking, sauces, and as marinade, and often rely heavily on an ingredient not found in Chinese dishes—coconut milk, which suffers the ignominy not only of being almost 90 percent fat by calories, but also of being one of the few non-animal foods which is rich in saturated fat—about 88 percent of the total fat is saturated, almost double that of beef!

Home-made Chinese

We, of course, can cure all of these maladies by making delicious Chinese food at home, using the water-sautéing method (page 11), which permits the flavors of a delicious assortment of fresh vegetables to strut their stuff, requiring only a small amount of pungent spices, such as ginger and mustard, to tickle the tongue. Soy sauce, either plain, low-salt, or tamari, is optional; reread the discussion on page 6, and if not used, go a little heavier on these others. If you do not choose to use soy sauce, taste first; remember that without sugar in the dish, a given amount of salt will come through much more strongly and that when virtually the entire rest of your cuisine is salt-free, you become much more sensitive to salt anyway. Also note that celery, as used in the fried rice, is somewhat higher in sodium than most vegetables, lending a bit of saltiness on its own.

About Brown Rice

Unless you are new to the healthful-eating scene, you are probably already familiar with brown rice; a brief discussion is given here for those who aren't, and some cooking advice is presented for those who think that cooking rice is hard.

I was about to start by saying that brown rice is simply white rice whose hull has not been removed, but wait a minute—which came first? It would be far more correct to say that white rice is brown rice whose hull *has* been removed, emphasizing that brown rice is the way that Nature grew it; and white rice is the unnatural, mutant derivative. Which have people been eating longer—what did humanity do before rice-milling machinery was available?

If you are scientifically-minded or a label-reader, such as I am, you may be surprised to find that white rice has a lower fat content than brown, because some of the essential oils are also lost in the milling. This doesn't imply that white rice is more healthful than brown; on the contrary, it simply proves my assertion that a diet of whole grains and vegetables provides all the fat (and protein, etc.) you need; you will suffer no "fat deficiency" and will be getting your small but essential daily fat requirement in the manner in which Nature intended, wrapped up in three times as much fiber and with the original vitamins and minerals, rather than a "vitamin pill" added in an attempt to replace what was lost in the milling.

The same point about fat content, incidentally, applies to whole wheat versus white flour, or to any other grain, for that matter, and explains why you do not need to eat wheat germ or to take wheat germ oil, etc. Why buy a car which has had the engine removed, and then go buy an engine, hoping it will fit properly, when you can get the complete package from the factory the way the engineer (or Engineer) designed it?

Rice Encounters

You may encounter both short- and long-grain brown rice, and perhaps medium, or maybe medium-long, or short-portly. (I take a 38 regular myself.) When I lived in Florida, long-grain was the only kind I saw; here in California, short-grain, grown locally, (in former deserts turned into rice paddies with taxpayer-subsidized water; end of political announcement) predominates, with long-grain available in places. They are virtually identical nutritionally; I find the short-grain to have a sweeter, nuttier, chewier taste and texture, with the long-grain having more of a distinct "rice" aroma and flavor. Throughout this book, the two varieties may be used interchangeably in any of the recipes, varying only the amount of water needed as in the recipe below; if you have both types available, try both to see if you have a favorite, or alternate for variety.

Because the water and steam have to penetrate and soften the tough outer hull, which is not present in white rice, brown rice takes much longer to cook than white, but it does so virtually unattended, so usually you can start the rice, make the rest of the recipe, and have your rice ready when the other ingredients are finished. In fact, if you have a time-programmable microwave, you can even put the rice in the oven, set the timer, and go to work or whatever, coming home to fresh, hot cooked rice. Nevertheless, I encourage you not to make less rice at one time than this recipes calls for, not because the recipe can't be cut in half easily (cut cooking time by about 10 minutes) but because the leftovers keep and reheat so well and make excellent bases for lunches. You have already seen several recipes in the Mexican section where leftover rice would be a great convenience, rather than having to cook it from scratch for an hour and *then* start the rest of the recipe.

To save leftovers, let rice cool and place in airtight plastic food-saver, or in bowl tightly covered with plastic wrap, and refrigerate for up to a week. To reheat, add a little water (about a tablespoon or two per cup) and microwave on "reheat" setting (70-80 percent), stirring once or twice, or simmer over low heat in a tightly covered saucepan, stirring a little more frequently and adding a little more water if needed to prevent burning, sticking, or drying out.

Here are the no-fail rice recipes and a nutritional analysis to use with recipes such as chili (page 20) in which the desired accompaniment, such as rice, must be added in separately, according to how much you choose to use.

Brown Rice

2 c. brown rice, any variety
4 c. water, if short-grain, 4 1/4 c.
water, if long-grain. For best and
quickest results, use hot tap
water.

To microwave: (*best!*) Place rice and water in 2-4 quart glass casserole dish with heavy, tight-fitting cover. Microwave on full power for 8 minutes, then on approximately 1/3 power (usually called "low," "defrost," "braise," etc.) for 52 minutes. (As mentioned above, this can be set in one step, even several hours in advance, with the programmable models.) Allow to sit, covered, for 5 minutes; then serve or use in recipe.

For stovetop: Place rice and water in 3-4 quart saucepan with tight-fitting lid. Bring to boil, stirring occasionally; then reduce heat to very low and cover tightly. Allow to steam, undisturbed, for 45-60 minutes (time will vary depending on just how high or low your "very low" is) until all water is absorbed. Removed from heat, allow to sit 5 minutes, still covered, fluff with fork, and serve.

P.S. If anyone ever tells you that you need salt in the water to cook rice, pasta, or any other grain, just throw their salt shaker at them. It does nothing for the cooking but give the addicts their indispensable salt-taste fix.

Yield: 6 cups or a little more of cooked rice. If used as the principal main dish, with, say, only low-calorie vegetables, serves 2-3; if accompanied by beans or more elaborate and substantial dishes such as chili, serves 2-6.

PER 1/4 RECIPE: 1/2 CUP RAW OR 1 1/2 CUP COOKIED

Protein 6g
Carbohydrates 66g
Fat...1.6g
Calories..306
Fat by Calories.............................4.7%

Fried Rice

1 recipe brown rice, cooked (see
above)
2 10-oz. packages frozen chopped
spinach
3 large ribs celery, chopped finely
3 bunches (about 15-25) green onions,
minus dark green tops, chopped
Soy sauce (optional)

Prepare rice and remove spinach from freezer, opening packages to allow it to thaw slightly. (If you are in a hurry, especially if your rice is left over or already prepared, you may thaw spinach gently in microwave while preparing other vegetables.) Clean and chop celery and onions. When rice is about 10 minutes from being done, sauté spinach, onions, and celery in *large* nonstick skillet (an electric skillet is ideal). Water will probably not be needed due to water given off as spinach finishes thawing. Continue cooking over moderate heat, breaking up spinach as it thaws and stirring occasionally. When spinach is thoroughly thawed and heated and other veggies are tender, add rice. (It is quite all right if rice has been sitting longer than the prescribed 5 minutes. In fact, leftover or precooked rice will work just fine, straight from the refrigerator.) Stir well, reduce heat slightly, cover, and cook 8-15 minutes, stirring frequently and adding a little water (and soy sauce, if desired) as needed to prevent sticking.

Yield: Serves 2-4

PER 1/4 RECIPE

Protein.. 11g
Carbohydrates............................. 77g
Fat...2.1g
Calories 366
Fat by Calories...........................5.3%

Chow Mein

For this staple of Chinese cookery (and takeout restaurants), of which no two versions are alike, each chef uses a different combination of vegetables, stir-fried quickly until tender-crisp. If you wonder why there are so few recipes in this chapter, that's why: because this one recipe is actually many. (Hey, that sounds pretty Orientally inscrutable, doesn't it?) There are so many possible combinations of vegetables that you could eat this the rest of your life (and should!) without duplicating the exact recipe, although you'll no doubt develop a favorite variation or two.

What I have done, then, is to give a general cooking method or guideline, plus a one-from-column-A-and-two-from-column-B approach. Listed below are three groupings of vegetables: those which are mandatory, in my humble opinion, and basic to the recipe; some others which I highly recommend, but which you may leave out if you don't like them or want variety; and the "optionals," of which you may add none, for a "quickie," or as many as you like. (If you add too many, they won't all fit in the skillet.)

Cleaning and cutting all those vegetables can be quite a job, so allow plenty of time—if I don't have a helper, I have to start *before* starting the rice—and make plenty, as the leftovers are delicious, and if you're going to that much trouble anyway, you might as well make lunch at the same time.

For pleasing visual and textural variety, cut vegetables into different shapes. Bok choy and the like are usually sliced diagonally; mushrooms can be sliced, quartered, or chopped into chunks; onions and peppers are often julienned (cut into long, thin strips); broccoli can be left in florets rather than cut; carrots can be cut into discs, strips, or spears, etc. Canned vegetables, such as bamboo shoots or water chestnuts, are often sold already conveniently sliced; baby corn should be left whole for a bright decorative touch. (Note: I have found that for some reason, Oriental vegetables come canned without salt much more often than their American counterparts.)

Due to the sheer quantity of vegetables, you'll need a large mixing bowl to store some of them while you prepare and cook others. Put the quickest-cooking and most delicate in the bowl first, so they get added to the skillet last. I suggest you separate bok choy leaves from the stalks, since the stalks take a while to cook and the leaves barely need to steam and can be added at the last minute. Start your skillet with the bok choy stalks, onions, and peppers, and any other thick raw vegetables, such as broccoli. Then add other fresh or frozen vegetables that require cooking, such as snow peas, one at a time. Canned goods such as bamboo shoots or baby corn are already cooked and do not need direct contact with the skillet (which by this time will be so full that they won't get it), so

they should be added after all the raw vegetables are in. Then, as mentioned, shredded greens such as the bok choy leaves can go on top of the heap.

Chow Mein Vegetable Suggestions

Basic

Mushrooms
Onions
Bok choy, celery, cabbage, or nappa, one or more
Bamboo shoots (canned)
Snow peas (China peas)

Recommended

Bean sprouts, preferably fresh
Water chesnuts (canned)
Green bell pepper
Carrot
Baby corn, canned

Optional

Broccoli
Red bell pepper
Zucchini
Scallions
Green beans, cut diagonally
Shiitake mushrooms, or other dried and reconstituted vegetables available at Oriental markets

Chow Mein Recipe

Fresh ginger, peeled and minced, or 1/2-2 tbsp. powdered ginger
1 tbsp. mustard seed (optional)
1-4 cloves garlic, minced (optional)
Vegetables, as above
Brown rice (page 27)

Place first few vegetables (see suggested list) in large skillet with large domed lid, such as an electric skillet. Add a bit of water, ginger, and garlic. Sauté over moderate heat—about 260°—stirring frequently. Do not wait for vegetables to cook thoroughly, or they will get overdone while new ones are cooking. Every minute or two, add another vegetable and stir, checking aroma to see if additional ginger is needed. If food starts to stick, add a bit more water and/or reduce heat. When all veggies are in pan, cover tightly and reduce heat. Allow to steam, stirring occasionally, a few minutes more until greens are done and all are hot and cooked.

To serve: Spoon over hot brown rice, with soy sauce on the side.

Yield: You've got to be kidding. It mostly depends on how big your skillet is. For a benchmark, though, I find that if I use 1/2 pound mushrooms, 1 large or 2 medium onions, 1 head of bok choy, 1/4 pound of snow peas, an 8-ounce can each (5 oz. drained) of bamboo shoots and water chestnuts, a 15-ounce can of baby corn, and 1 large or 2 small carrots, and serve it with 1 recipe brown rice, it serves 2-6. More of the optional vegetables, or a higher rice-to-veggie ratio, will increase this.

Nutritional data: This will also obviously depend on type and quantity of vegetables selected. But whatever you choose, it will be almost all carbohydrate, virtually fat-free, and the lower- and higher-calorie vegetables will probably average out to something less than 100 calories per pound of raw vegetables in the total mix. In fact, the low fat content and high fiber and water content of these veggies are responsible for the old joke which was satirized in the subheading for this chapter. The dish *is* very filling, with very low calorie content, so you end up leaving the table without having ingested a lot of calories (unless you go heavy on the rice). Ideal for dieters! Anyway, here's an analysis based on the sample recipe listed under Yield. Don't forget to add the values for the appropriate quantity of rice per serving, from the chart on page 27.

PER 1/4 RECIPE

Protein 9g
Carbohydrates 39g
Fat 1.2g
Calories...176
Fat by Calories...........................6.25%

Variations: (1) If you like a thicker sauce, mix 1-2 tablespoons cornstarch with some of the broth from the skillet, adding water if necessary to form a smooth paste. Add this mix to skillet during last few minutes of cooking; stir well to coat all veggies and allow to cook to desired thickness, adding more water as required.

(2) If someone in the house is still in the last throes of sugar addiction, throw in a few chunks of fresh or juice-packed canned pineapple during the last few minutes of cooking or mix in while serving or serve on the side. If using the cornstarch sauce as described above, use the juice from the canned pineapple as part of the mixing liquid. A sweet-and-sour effect can be achieved by adding 2-4 tablespoons of vinegar also.

Personally, I prefer to eat my dessert separately from my dinner.

Lo Mein

Chinese restaurants stir-fry their noodles in oil to make their lo mein, but you don't have to. Just choose your favorite pasta from the discussion in the next chapter on Italian cooking, prepare according to package directions, and serve the chow mein veggies over the hot cooked noodles. For this purpose I heartily recommend the slight cross-cultural clash of using a Japanese product known as soba noodles, which are a mixture of buckwheat and whole wheat. When served in a large bowl with veggies and ample broth, the resulting dish is called udon.

Incidentally, I have found little of vegetarian appeal in Japanese restaurants or cuisine. Salt is the predominant flavor, in pickles, marinades, and soy products such as miso; main dishes are more fish than vegetable oriented; and many, such as tempura, are deep-fried. But I'm grateful for the soba noodles, which are carried by most health-food stores and some supermarkets.

Now let's do as Marco Polo did, and go (back) from China to Italy!

Chapter 6: Italian

When the Moon Hits Your Eye Like a Big Veggie Pie, That's Amore!

While I was writing this book, I came across a column by Erma Bombeck. Complaining, as she often does, of the impossibility of losing weight while eating garbage, she bewailed the fact that she had never seen a low-calorie pot of spaghetti sauce bubbling on the stove. I was tempted to send her my recipe for some, but thought, No, she's sold enough books, let her buy a copy of mine!

Nowadays, many people know better than to consider pastas as fattening foods—in fact, they're becoming something of a rage among carbo-loading runners, waistline-conscious yuppies, and gourmands who douse them in olive oil with duck sausage or lox (probably only in Los Angeles). But this last points up the same truth brought out regarding potatoes (see page 14)—the pasta itself isn't fattening; it's what you put on it that makes the difference. Spaghetti sauce loaded with greasy beef and oil and topped with fatty cheese isn't going to do your waistline *or* your arteries any good. But this doesn't mean that the Ermas of the world need give up their favorite Italian dishes. On the contrary, with a little vegetarian magic, not only spaghetti, but lasagna, minestrone, and even "sausage" submarines become healthful, low-calorie fare, suitable for anyone's diet, and every bit as satisfying as the stuff they peddle at Dino's (or wherever).

The "trick," as everywhere else, is to let the flavors of wheat, mushrooms, tomatoes, eggplant, and other vegetables come through in their fullest glory, rather than being smothered by a blanket of fat and salt (commonly known as cheese), as is their usual fate. While lasagna or submarines without cheese may at first sound as unlikely as a cheeseless burrito, it comes out just as well—it will taste *different* the first time you try it, and *better* than the old way the second time, especially if you've been eating the other recipes in this book and started losing your taste for fat and salt.

About Pastas

What an exciting adventure awaits you the first time you wander away from the supermarket semolina and into the pasta section of a good natural-foods store! Face it—white spaghetti, like the white flour it's made from, has very little taste, which is why it seems to require rich, fatty sauces to have any appeal. But here you'll find pastas made not only of whole-wheat flour, but with buckwheat, spinach, carrots, varied grains and their sprouts, and even some exotic (and possibly unknown to you) ingredients such as amaranth flour. And, as long as you READ THE LABELS carefully, they'll all provide you with the same health benefits— low fat, low sodium, high fiber—while offering a variety of tastes, textures, and appearances to make your cooking anything but dull, not only gastronomically but visually as well.

31

What are you reading the label for? The biggest offender is eggs, found even in "health-food" sections, most often in noodles rather than spaghetti—that is, in items such as fettucini, lasagna, and spinach noodles. Other things to watch out for are white flour (semolina or others), salt, and oils. This isn't even a matter of compromising—none of these are necessary, and there are many products available that contain none. Some are as simple as a whole-wheat spaghetti which contains only whole-wheat flour and nothing else. (Wait a minute, they had to add water to make it into dough.) At the other extreme, one of my favorites, especially in soups, is an elbow pasta, multi-colored, whose list of ingredients reads as follows: organically grown whole-wheat flour, wheat germ, seven sprouted whole grains (wheat, barley, oats, triticale, corn, rye, millet), dry onion, dry celery, dry spinach, dry tomato. Whew! With all those colors and flavors, who could ever go back to plain white spaghetti? And who needs salt or grease on top of it?

In addition to the varied ingredients and tastes, you'll find an assortment of shapes which also rivals that of the supermarket pastas. Regular thick and thin spaghetti (vermicelli), lasagna noodles, corkscrews, seashells, elbows, macaroni, ziti, you name it—just about any mold which has been used to press out conventional pasta has been used on the healthful stuff too.

Experiment around with the different types (what a fun way to experiment, huh?) in any dish you like. I've listed a few of my favorites below, and the dishes in which I often use them, to get you started. But please don't feel restricted to these or to these uses. Try any product which meets the guidelines above, in any dish you want—if you start with good ingredients, how could the result be bad? Anyway, here are some to look for:

• Whole-wheat spaghetti. The basic stuff, made from the flour alone. A good starter for plain spaghetti dishes, but I like to alternate it with the others, especially:

• Buckwheat spaghetti. May also be called soba—see page 29. This is actually my favorite for spaghetti-and-mushroom-sauce.

• Amaranth spaghetti. Whole wheat mixed with amaranth flour. The manufacturer makes all kinds of mystical claims for amaranth, a South American grain. I don't believe a word of them, but it's good,

nonetheless.

• Lasagna. Made with whole wheat, of course.

• Spinach lasagna. Adds a little color to the lasagna noodles.

• Elbow pasta. This can be plain, or colored like the product I described above. I like it in soups and stews for the color it adds.

• Twists, seashells, corkscrews, with and without spinach (watch out for eggs!). Great as a base for pasta primavera, as they provide texture to keep the vegetables from slipping off your plate.

There are many others, and the inventory may change each time you go in the store. If within the guidelines, they'll all be similar nutritionally, and cooking instructions will vary only in length of time. Enjoy.

P.S. No, I don't particularly need the wheat germ which is listed in the ingredients of the multigrain elbows, above, but the amount is so small that it still stays within the fat guidelines, at only 1 gram per 2-ounce serving.

How to Cook Pasta

How could it be any easier? Boil 4-5 quarts of water in an 8-quart or larger pot. Add pasta carefully, to prevent breaking. Continue a rolling boil over very high heat. Stir frequently to prevent sticking. Test by chewing a piece a minute or two before the time given on the package. Continue testing every minute or so until desired degree of tenderness is reached—the standard, of course, is al dente (literally, "to the tooth"), or a bit chewy. When done, pour into colander. Running some cold tap water in the sink will help to keep the steam from peeling your wallpaper. Rinse with cold tap water, both to prevent sticking and to stop cooking—otherwise, it may get mushy, especially the later servings. Don't worry about the fact that this will cool off the pasta—your piping-hot sauce will reheat it more than amply. Drain well and serve.

If later servings have gotten a bit sticky or cold, run some hot tap water briefly over spaghetti in colander and drain well, separating pasta with your fingers.

Now don't you feel silly for all those times you put oil and salt into your boiling water for pasta?

Leftover pasta is best kept separately from its sauce, to prevent mushiness upon reheating. Drain well and place in airtight plastic container or a bowl tightly covered with plastic wrap. Allow sauce to cool and store in covered container. Reheat sauce in microwave or over low heat on stovetop, stirring frequently. Place desired quantity of leftover pasta in colander, run hot tap water over it, drain well and serve.

Nutritional data: Will vary a bit depending on added ingredients, such as other grains, spinach, etc. But as long as you buy those without added fats (eggs, oil, shortening), you can figure on about 100 calories and 1 gram of fat (don't buy it if it has any more than that) per uncooked ounce.

Spaghetti With Mushroom Sauce

I should probably call this my Erma Bombeck Special, in honor of her column referred to at the beginning of the chapter, and dedicate it to all those who thought dieting meant living on celery sticks forever. Chow down, O ye of ample girth; skip the garlic bread, if you wish, but don't forget a big tossed salad—with a celery stick or two, perhaps—and enjoy this low-fat, low-calorie, incredibly satisfying dish.

1 lb. fresh mushrooms
1 very large or 2 medium onions, cut
    in strips
4-10 cloves garlic (don't be bashful!),
    crushed
2 large cans (28-30 oz.) tomato purée
1/2-1 tbsp. onion powder
1/2-1 tbsp. or more garlic powder
1-2 tbsp. or more oregano
1 tbsp. or more basil
1 tbsp. or more marjoram
1-3 whole bay leaves
1/2-1 tbsp. rosemary
Pinch crushed hot red pepper (pizza
    type)

Wipe mushrooms clean with paper towel (do not rinse). Cut off woody stem ends if necessary and cut mushrooms in varied shapes—slice some, quarter others. Do not chop too finely; they provide the texture.

Sauté mushrooms, onions, and garlic in water as needed in 5-6 quart saucepan until tender. Add purée and spices. Be generous

with herbs; we're skipping the salt and oil, so we want these flavors. The red pepper is optional but highly desirable—the idea here is *not* to taste the pepper or make a "hot" sauce, but only to liven up the flavor of everything else, so only a pinch is needed.

Bring to a simmer over moderate heat, stirring frequently. Reduce heat and simmer covered, stirring occasionally, for one or more hours, up to all day, or make in advance and reheat as for chili (page 20). Serve over your favorite pasta with a tossed salad, and, if you wish, garlic bread (recipe later).

Yield: Again, will depend on sauce-to-spaghetti ratio and on whether served with garlic bread. With bread, I find that 1 pound of pasta plus sauce serves 4-8, with sometimes a bit of sauce left over, sometimes not, depending on how heavy you like it sauced.

Note: In addition to refrigerating as above, sauce can be frozen for longer-term storage, say up to six months, in airtight containers. Reheated sauce can be used not only over pasta, but also on rice, potatoes, bread of any kind, vegetables, etc.

Nutritional data: Add in figures for proper amount of pasta you are using from package or from representative datum on this page.

PER 1/8 RECIPE

Protein	11g
Carbohydrates	51g
Fat	0.6g
Calories	118
Fat by Calories	4.8%

Variation: HIGHLY RECOMMENDED. Core and chop coarsely 1 very large or 2 medium ripe beefsteak tomatoes. Add to sauce with purée and spices. Provides additional texture and a different type of tomato flavor from that of the purée; for you obsessive-compulsive types, add a whopping 6 calories per serving to the above figures.

Spaghetti and "Meatballs"

For spaghetti and "meatballs," prepare one recipe shamburgers (page 14), but add 1/2 tablespoon oregano, basil, marjoram, and rosemary to chopped eggplant while it cooks. Form into balls instead of burgers; pan-fry or broil as in burger recipe, turning more frequently due to round instead of flat shape. Place cooked balls on top of pasta and pour sauce over all.

Note: This will make a much more filling dish and so will serve more than the sauce-only recipe. Sixteen meatballs would give 94 calories per meatball; with 1 1/2-2 pounds of pasta you should be able to serve 8, or even more if bread is served also.

Variation: Because the meatballs provide texture and flavor, you may, if you wish, omit the mushrooms from this version, making it even more of a change from the first recipe.

Lasagna

1 8- or 12-oz. package whole wheat or
    spinach lasagna noodles
1 large can tomato purée
1-2 tsp. onion powder
2-3 tsp. garlic powder
2-3 tsp. oregano
1-2 tsp. marjoram
1-2 tsp. basil
1 medium eggplant, about 1 lb. or so
1 lb. zucchini, sliced
2 10-oz. packages frozen spinach,
    thawed and drained

Cook noodles according to package directions; rinse, drain, and allow to cool. While waiting for noodle water to boil, place tomato purée and spices in 2-quart saucepan. Bring to slow boil, reduce heat, cover and simmer, stirring occasionally, until ready to use.

Pierce whole eggplant in several places with a fork. Microwave on full power 6-10 minutes, turning halfway through, until not quite tender, or bake in 350° oven 30-40 minutes. Allow to cool, then slice about a quarter inch thick.

Spoon a little sauce in bottom of large, deep casserole. Place a layer of noodles over bottom, trimming to shape and using trimmings jigsaw-fashion as needed, then cover with eggplant slices. Spoon sauce over, add a layer of noodles, then spread spinach over dish. Add sauce, noodles, and zucchini slices, then sauce, noodles, and final topping of sauce.

Microwave, covered, on about 2/3 power ("Bake" or "Roast") for 30-40 minutes or until heated through and bubbly, or bake in

350° oven 40-60 minutes.

To serve: Remove from heat and let stand 10 minutes. Cut through noodles with a sharp knife into serving-size squares. Spoon out sauce from bottom of casserole and pour a little over each slice. Serve with a tossed salad. Refrigerate leftovers in original covered casserole, or for smaller portions, on plate or bowl tightly covered with plastic wrap. Microwaving is best way to reheat; for oven or stovetop reheating, add water and use low heat for a long period of time, so steam can penetrate to inner layers.

Yield: I find that with a 12-ounce box of noodles, I usually end up discarding some (or saving for a lunch with leftover spaghetti sauce), so unless you have a really big casserole, use these figures for an 8-ounce package of pasta. Serves 2-4; garlic bread, of course, would stretch.

PER 1/4 RECIPE

Protein 18g
Carbohydrates 72g
Fat 3.1g
Calories 353
Fat by Calories 8%

Sausage Subs

Be honest, now, did you ever really think that you'd find sausage subs in a diet-and-health book? Surprise, surprise!

Reread the discussion of hamburger buns on page 13, and look for sub rolls meeting the same guidelines. Shortly after I discovered the burger buns made with sprouted wheat, which I mentioned in that section, I found that the same company also makes "hot dog" or sub rolls from the exact same recipe, with the same nutritional data. Perfect! Again, if you can't find anything that isn't fat-laden, use genuine French sourdough sub rolls from the supermarket, reading the label to make sure they contain only flour, water, and salt.

Sausages:
1 recipe shamburgers (page 14) but
    add to the chopped eggplant
    while it cooks:
3 tbsp. fennel seed
1 tsp. (for mild sausage) to 1 tbsp. or

more (for hot sausage) crushed
red pepper flakes

Sauce:
1 green bell pepper
1 red bell pepper
1 large onion
1 tsp. garlic powder
1 tsp. onion powder
1 tsp. oregano
1 tsp. rosemary

Prepare sausage filling. While it cools, core, rib, and seed peppers. Slice peppers and onion into long, thin strips. Water-sauté in medium saucepan, browning onions as much as possible without sticking or burning. When peppers are tender (about 5-10 minutes; if they are not tender enough it can be speeded up by covering pot and/or adding more water), add tomato purée and spices. Simmer, covered, stirring occasionally, while proceeding with sausages.

When sausage mixture is cool, shape into 8 long sausages, about 1-2" thick. They will probably come out more square than round—that's OK; it makes for easier cooking. Do *not* season outside as for shamburgers. Broil or pan-fry as for shamburgers, turning 3 times so all four sides get crisp and browned.

When sausages are done, preheat oven to 350°. Cover baking sheet with aluminum foil. Split buns and place on sheet. Put a little sauce on each half, spreading it to cover bun. Place a sausage in middle and spread more sauce on top. Cover with aluminum foil, tightly sealed, and bake for 15 minutes or until heated through. For crisp buns, remove foil cover last 5 minutes. (Since this dries the sauce a bit, you may have to add a tad more sauce before serving.) Or, bake or broil buns by themselves; then add sauce, sausage, sauce, and serve. (I prefer the first method because the sauce permeates the buns, making a fine, gooey mess.)

To serve: Place on plate with a knife and fork crossed on top of sub. Anyone who attempts to pick up sub and eat with his fingers has to clean up the entire dining room, kitchen, bathroom, and do the dishes, besides.

Yield: 8 subs, serving 4-8.

PER SUB

Protein	7g
Carbohydrates	52g
Fat	1.8g
Calories	240
Fat by Calories	6.8%

Note: Add values for buns you have chosen. Typical 125-calorie bun, then, would equal 365 calories per sub. And just as gooey a delight as the cheese-laden, 1,000-calorie grease bombs at the local pizza joint!

Eggplant Subs

This is a different taste and texture from the sausage subs, a lot less work, and, if you're really on a warp-speed diet, a lot fewer calories as well.

Prepare sausage sub sauce, above, adding a pinch of crushed red pepper. Pierce 2 medium eggplants with a fork and microwave on full power for 10-15 minutes, turning once, or until tender all the way through, or bake whole in 350° oven 30-45 minutes. (Make sure they're thoroughly done.) Broil or warm buns, add sauce, slice eggplant and layer slices on buns, top with sauce and serve. Makes 8 subs.

PER SUB (ADD BUN VALUES)

Protein	3g
Carbohydrates	17g
Fat	0.5g
Calories	75(!)
Fat by Calories	6%

Pasta Primavera

This dish, which tops pasta with tender-crisp vegetables instead of purée-based sauces, has become quite popular in trendy, chic restaurants, many or most of which are not "Italian." Our non-fat, low-cal version has a lot of flavor and "crunch," especially with my recommended seashell pasta (see page 32). For greater visual appeal, set the veggies on top of "substitute" shells made with artichoke flour (and, unfortunately, semolina or white flour), whose white color allows the green, orange, red, and brown toppings to stand out.

Don't be bashful with the fresh garlic garnish—it livens up the entire dish. (See page 44 for a discussion of the same thing regarding raw onions.) Here, instead of blending many spices as in most of the recipes, we concentrate on just two, basil and garlic, so let them "do their thing!"

1 lb. fresh mushrooms
2 lb. ripe tomatoes
10 oz. frozen or fresh broccoli
10 oz. frozen or fresh cauliflower
    (about 1/2 of a head—exact
      amount is not critical)
2 large or 3 medium carrots
6 or more garlic cloves, divided
Basil
1 lb. pasta of choice (see discussion)

Start pasta water boiling. Clean mushrooms and quarter, slice thickly or chop coarsely. When water boils, plunge tomatoes into it for 8-12 seconds, depending on size; then place under cold running water. (This makes them incredibly easy to peel.) Peel, core, and chop tomatoes coarsely. (Keep the water covered to save the heat—you'll need it boiling again soon.) Cut broccoli and cauliflower into florets. Peel carrots and cut into about 2-inch lengths, then quarter lengthwise to make spears. Peel all garlic cloves. Bring water back to boil.

Place tomatoes in 2-quart saucepan with 2 tablespoons or more basil and 2 crushed garlic cloves. Bring to boil over medium heat, reduce heat, cover, and simmer, stirring occasionally, about 10 minutes. At same time, place mushrooms, broccoli, cauliflower, carrots, and 2 more crushed garlic cloves in nonstick electric or other skillet. Cook over low heat (about 260-280°) covered, stirring frequently, about 10 minutes or until tender-crisp (except the mushrooms, of course!). If you cover tightly to save the steam you may not need to add any water.

Put pasta in water either just before or just after starting tomatoes and veggies, depending on cooking time recommended on package.

To serve: Put hot, drained pasta on plate. Top with tomatoes and sprinkle additional basil on top. Add veggies, scattering around different varieties for color appeal. Squeeze garlic in press over each portion to each person's taste. Do not allow anyone to wimp out.

Because of the lack of liquid sauce, this dish will not reheat quite as well as most. Unused portions may be refrigerated with all ingredients together, and microwaved or reheated gently on stovetop, covered.

Variations: Add any one of the following: fresh or frozen asparagus, green beans (regular or Italian), or frozen peas. (Too many additions will make it too "busy" and overwhelm the taste of the pasta.)

Yield: Serves 2-4, or more if stretched with salad and rolls.

PER 1/4 RECIPE

Protein	25g
Carbohydrates	105g
Fat	3.1g
Calories	503
Fat by Calories	5.5%

Minestrone

What could be better than a hot bowl of thick, hearty soup on a cold day? (If you live in Miami or environs, read "on an over-air-conditioned day"—a common occurrence.) And for once, "hearty" means good for your heart, instead of the opposite, as it usually does. Yes, soups can be thickened with healthful complex carbohydrates from beans and pasta, instead of oil, ham hock fat, or refined flours. And, of course, this keeps the calorie count down for the dieters.

While minestrone certainly makes an appetizing first course for any Italian meal (and a lot of others, as well), I like it as the star attraction at dinner. With some crusty garlic bread (don't worry, I'll get there!) and a tossed salad, it's a complete meal with a wonderful variety of tastes and textures. It takes a bit of time to make, but the recipe makes ample, so refrigerate any leftovers—it's another one of those that seems to get even better upon reheating—and use for lunches, an appetizer for another night's dinner, or a second, no-work dinner, giving you a night off from the kitchen. (Yes, even we dedicated chefs appreciate that once in a while!) Refrigerate the soup in the original pot, if there's a lot, or in plastic storage containers, or freeze for several months in airtight freezer containers. Either way, reheat (or thaw) very slowly, in microwave or in a covered saucepan, adding a little water if the soup has thickened too much, and stirring frequently.

As I've mentioned in discussing pasta, my favorite for this soup is a sprouted-grain, multi-colored elbow pasta. My second favorite is whole-wheat twists. Both varieties add texture and color. Experiment with any pastas you like.

4-6 c. water, divided
1 16-oz. can navy beans, drained
1 16-oz. can kidney beans, drained
    (brands may vary from 15-19 oz.)
2 large carrots, peeled and sliced into
    discs
2 large onions, peeled and sliced
3 large celery ribs, chopped coarsely
2 16-oz. cans tomatoes, *undrained* and
    chopped
2-6 cloves garlic, chopped
Oregano
Basil
Sage
Rosemary
Marjoram
Parsley
Garlic powder
Onion powder
6 oz. uncooked pasta (see discussion)
1 10-oz. package frozen Italian green
    beans

Place navy beans in blender with 2 cups water and purée until smooth. Place in 6-quart or larger soup pot with 2 more cups water, kidney beans, carrots, onions, celery, garlic, tomatoes, and *generous* amounts of all seasonings. Bring to boil, reduce heat, cover, and simmer, stirring occasionally, 1 hour or until carrots and celery are tender. Uncover, return to boil, and add pasta. Boil, stirring occasionally, as directed on pasta package, until pasta is tender. (Note: may take a bit longer than package says.) Reduce heat, add green beans, cover and simmer until beans are tender—about another 10-15 minutes. Soup will be very thick—you may add up to 2 cups additional water at any time during cooking, if you like, or even more if you want a thinner soup. (That would be OK for an appetizer. For dinner, keep it pretty thick.) Serve piping hot.

Yield: Makes 18-20 cups. As an appetizer, serves 10-20; as a main dish without bread, serves 3-6; with bread (and a salad), 4-8.

PER 1/4 RECIPE

Protein	19g
Carbohydrates	91g
Fat	2.3g
Calories	468
Fat by Calories	4.5%

PER CUP (APPROX.)

Protein	4g
Carbohydrates	20g
Fat	0.5g
Calories	104
Fat by Calories	Same

Only 312 calories for six dieters! You will find it filling and, like almost all soups, emotionally satisfying as well.

Garlic Bread

This is a vital (to my mind) accompaniment to minestrone. It is also occasionally desirable with spaghetti or even lasagna, as a change in taste and texture. I also use it to stretch a favorite recipe, perhaps for company.

Reread the discussion of hamburger buns (page 13), but this time expand your search in the health-food store to include rolls, such as squaw rolls and others which are presented as dinner rolls. READ THE LABELS. You will almost surely find one or several which meet our guidelines—if not, back to your trusty (but white flour) sourdough rolls. Yes, you could make your own (and more power to you if you do), but who's got time these days, especially since creating gourmet meals from vegetables and grains admittedly takes a lot more time than throwing a steak under the broiler?

Speaking of saving time, I'll give you three methods—an ultra-quick method, if you're really pressed for time or laden with other cooking chores, a standard method, and a gourmet variation. They all produce slightly different flavors, so try all three on different occasions (or, for that matter, on the same occasion, if you've got the time and are a scientific type who likes to compare).

Ultra-quick method: Preheat oven to 350°. Line baking sheet with foil (for quick clean-up). Place rolls on foil. Brush tops with water (to help hold spices). Sprinkle with garlic powder, oregano, basil, marjoram—as much as will stay on rolls. (What falls off will steam and release some flavor, too, so don't clean it off.) Cover loosely with additional foil, crimping edges tightly to make a "tent." Bake 15 minutes or until thoroughly heated. For crisp rolls, remove cover last 5 minutes or more and continue baking to desired crispness. Keep additional servings warm by resealing in foil and returning to oven, with oven heat shut off. Refrigerate or freeze leftovers, tightly wrapped in foil, and reheat in microwave or by adding a few drops of water and reheating in oven, sealed in foil, at 350°.

Yield: As an accompaniment to soup or spaghetti, I allow two average-size rolls per person; light eaters may need only one.

Standard method: Crush fresh garlic in press and spread over tops of rolls with knife. Do not brush with water. Add seasonings and cook as above.

Gourmet method: Place entire head of garlic on foil in 350° oven for 15-30 minutes, turning occasionally and removing any cloves which start to brown, until all cloves are soft. Scrape creamy garlic paste off skin with a knife and spread over rolls. Add seasonings and cook as above. Yum!

Variations: Whole-wheat English muffins or bagels are tasty substitutes for rolls. Split and top each half with garlic and seasonings as in any of the three methods. (You may also use this split method on regular rolls—it *does* make it easier to keep the spices on the roll; no water is needed.)

The split method offers an additional taste and texture variation by broiling the seasoned open faces, instead of baking. Place on foil, season, and broil on second rack to desired crispness. If you like a crisp outer crust all around, *plus* a toasted surface, bake split halves uncovered; OR bake covered, then place under broiler.

Pizza

O happy day, when health-food makers began making prebaked pizza crusts, thus saving us hours of time and mess raising and rolling dough which took a lot less time to eat than to make! I recently came across

crusts made with no oil or shortening what-soever, made only of ground wheat sprouts, honey (oh, well, you can't have everything), water, yeast, and salt. (Notice there's less salt than yeast.) They're sold refrigerated or frozen (and should be kept frozen if not used very quickly, since there are no preserv-atives), and can be popped out of the fridge as is, topped, and thrown in the oven for a very low-fuss pizza. I should add that they're delicious as well. The ground wheat sprouts have much more flavor than the convention-al oily, white-flour dough.

If you cannot find such creations at your local purveyors, you are not doomed to a piz-zaless existence (or worse, to eating the grease-discs at you-know-who's corner joint). Not only health-food stores, but often super-markets, carry whole-wheat pita breads, which are made without shortening and even without honey, consisting of only flour, water, and salt. (READ THE LABEL. A few brands may add oil.) These can be split and topped to produce a thin-crust pie.

If you get really desperate (or just want a change), you can put the pizza toppings on split whole-wheat English muffins, bagels, or even any of our burger buns, sub rolls, or sourdough rolls, but you'll be getting away from the pizza-like appearance, taste, and texture.

Whatever you use, though, it will be good and will retrieve for you another treat you thought you'd have to give up when you decided to eat sensibly!

**2 10 -inch pizza crusts or large whole-
    wheat pitas (see discussion)**
1 28-oz. can tomato purée
Garlic powder
Onion powder
Oregano
Basil
Marjoram
1 medium onion, sliced thinly
**1 green bell pepper, cored, ribbed,
    and seeded, sliced into thin rings**
1/4 lb. fresh mushrooms, sliced thinly
2-6 cloves garlic, crushed

Preheat oven to 400°. For crisp crust, use thawed crusts; for softer crust, use directly from freezer.

Simmer tomato purée with 1 teaspoon to 1 tablespoon of each spice, to taste. While it simmers, clean and prepare vegetables. Spread sauce on crust; then add onions, peppers, and mushrooms. Sprinkle crushed garlic over top; then sprinkle additional oregano over all. Bake directly on baking sheet about 10-15 minutes, or until veggies are cooked and crust is to desired crispness. For extra-crisp crust, preheat baking sheet; for extra-soft, use foil on top of baking sheet. Cut into 4 or 6 slices and serve. Keep remaining portions warm in turned-off oven, covered with foil to prevent further crisping (unless, of course, you *want* further crisping).

Yield: Serves 2-4; would be more likely to serve more than 2 if accompanied by a tossed salad.

Variations: Add any or all of the following before cooking: Sliced tomatoes, sliced zucchini, crushed red pepper flakes, sliced red bell pepper, or just about any other thinly-sliced vegetable you can think of!

Note: If you have leftover sauce, freeze for future pizzas, throw in your next batch of spaghetti sauce, or use for lunches as suggested with spaghetti sauce (page 33).

Nutritional data: Based on 2 10-inch (total 1 pound) crusts which total: 48g/240g/4.8g/1164 calories. Substitute values for crusts or bread you use.

PER 1/4 RECIPE (1/2 PIZZA)

Protein... 16g
Carbohydrates............................... 82g
Fat..1.7g
Calories 391
Fat by Calories.............................. 4%

And now, let's continue moving east, perhaps sailing the Mediterranean if we wish to avoid Hannibal coming across the Alps!

Chapter 7: French/Spanish/ Mediterranean/Creole

Cook It and You'll Basque in Praise! (Sorry)

Continuing east on our culinary trip around the world, we now journey into realms where the exact geographic and cultural ownership of a given dish is somewhat less exact. The French cooking referred to, of course, is not the *haute cuisine* of Paris and the Cordon Bleu school (whose theory is that no matter how bad something is, if you cover it with enough butter, flour and cream, most people will think it's good), but rather the more down-to-earth dishes of the peasants and shepherds of the mountains or eastern coasts.

Ratatouille

Popular throughout the Mediterranean, there are almost as many versions of this dish as there are cooks. This one (aside from being fat- and oil-free, of course) is quick, easy, tasty, and different from everything else in this book.

I must mention that this is another dish of fantastic visual appeal. Red, yellow, green, purple, beige, and tan—the colors dazzle the eye. Even a touch such as the cutting of the peppers into squares instead of the usual strips lends visual as well as textural variety.

With this recipe, cooking indeed becomes an *art*!

2 c. raw brown rice
1/2 lb. fresh mushrooms
1 medium eggplant, about 1 lb., unpeeled
1/2 lb. summer squash (yellow or crookneck)
1/2 lb. zucchini (If either squash or zucchini is unavailable, use 1 lb. of the other.)
1 red bell pepper
1 green bell pepper
2-6 cloves garlic
1 large or 2 medium tomatoes, very ripe (about 3/4-1 lb.)
Oregano
Basil
Parsley flakes
Cumin
Dash or two of cinnamon

Wipe mushrooms clean, discarding woody stem ends if necessary; cut into quarters or very large chunks; then start rice. (Otherwise rice will be done well before veggies are cooked. However, if you have a helper, go ahead and start rice; then start cleaning veggies.) If you are going to microwave veggies, which I highly recommend for easy cleanup as well as maximum flavor, use stovetop method for rice (page 27)—unless, of course, you have two large microwave ovens; you lucky dog, you.

Clean eggplant, squash, and zucchini, and cut into approximately 1/2" cubes, or a little larger. Core, seed, and rib peppers and cut into 1" squares. Peel and chop garlic fairly fine, but in still discernible pieces. Core tomato and cut into 1/2" cubes.

Mix all vegetables in large, deep, covered casserole dish (and preheat oven to 350°, if used). Add all spices, using 1-2 teaspoons except for cinnamon (just a few shakes). Mix well; then add spices again, in about same amount or to taste.

Microwave, covered, for about 20-30 minutes on full power, stirring very well once, or until eggplant is thoroughly done. (Check eggplant after 20 minutes and then periodically; undercooked eggplant is blecch.) Or bake, covered, at 350° for 40-60 minutes, stirring once, using same test.

To serve: As soon as vegetables are done, serve over portions of hot cooked rice. (It is OK if rice finishes a bit early. It will keep hot in its dish or pot.) With all of these vegetables, ratatouille is a complete meal in itself and needs no accompaniment. Note: Be sure to ladle some of the broth from the bottom of the casserole over each portion!

Yield: Serves 2-4.

PER 1/4 RECIPE

Protein 12g
Carbohydrates............................. 87g
Fat 2.4g
Calories 406
Fat by Calories............................5.3%

Potatoes Nicoise

Most chefs would be hard pressed to quote the multiple sources which eventually gave rise to their favorite recipes; even those which are "original" are based on items or cooking methods learned elsewhere. After all, just as all composers use the same twelve notes, with the genius being in the arranging therein, all chefs use the same available list of edible foods, applying their own unique touches thereto.

In the case of this recipe, however, the direct inspiration was so great that I must give credit to *American Wholefoods Cuisine* (Nikki and David Goldbeck, 1983: New American Library, N.Y.) for the basic idea. It required a vegetarian such as myself, though, to create cooking methods and spicing to show that this delicious dish can indeed be made, and even made better,

without the fatty ingredients and salt.

The ultra-lean result is delicious for everyone and a special boon to dieters, (even more so than most vegetarian dishes) being especially filling in only a 381-calorie dinner.

2-6 cloves garlic, crushed
3 lbs. large baking potatoes, cleaned
but not peeled
2 large or 3 medium Bermuda (red)
onions, about 1 1/2-2 lbs.
2 lbs. ripe tomatoes
3 tsp. thyme, or more to taste
3 tsp. basil, or more to taste
4 tbsp. parsley flakes

Spray a nonstick electric or other skillet with nonstick vegetable spray. Spread crushed garlic over surface of skillet. Slice potatoes about an eighth-inch thick and layer half of them in skillet (you'll probably make two layers with each half). Slice onions fairly thinly and cover potatoes with one layer of onions. Slice tomatoes slightly thicker than potatoes—three-sixteenth inch or a little more—and add one layer of tomatoes, covering dish completely. Sprinkle half of each seasoning over all. Layer remaining potatoes, one more layer of onions, and one more layer of tomatoes. Cover with remaining seasonings. Cover skillet very tightly and set to 240°, or on low heat. (If using a conventional stovetop without temperature control, check occasionally and turn down heat if steam starts escaping heavily.) Cook for about 1 hour or until potatoes are completely tender.

Note: Allow plenty of time for slicing and assembly, about 45 minutes to an hour. However, dish can cook virtually unattended, making it not so time consuming in the long run.

To serve: Cut into sixths, eights, or ninths, with the edge of a nylon spatula (to avoid scratching skillet). Lift out carefully and push with flat side of knife so it slides off spatula and onto plate, keeping layers and cube shape intact. Cut each bite from the top to bottom with sharp knife so you get some of each layer in every bite. Be sure to spoon a little of broth from skillet over each serving. Keep remaining servings warm in tightly covered skillet on "warm" setting.

Despite the relatively small number of ingredients (for a vegetarian dish), I find the abundance of tastes and textures in this dish don't seem to require an accompaniment. If you wish one, however, cooked fresh or frozen broccoli will provide good color, taste, and sensory complementation.

Refrigerate leftovers on plate or in bowl, tightly covered with plastic wrap (*and* aluminum foil, if you like to minimize any onion and spice smell in your refrigerator). Reheat on microwave dish or bowl, covered with plastic wrap (if you've been clever, the same ones in which you stored it), on medium power, turning frequently. It is best to cut into separate portions before reheating, else you will have to cut the square apart and rotate insides to outsides during reheating. Or reheat in tightly covered saucepan on stove over low heat, with a few drops of water added as needed to produce steam to penetrate dish.

Yield: Serves 2-4.

PER 1/4 RECIPE

Protein	12g
Carbohydrates	85g
Fat	1g
Calories	381
Fat by Calories	2.3%

Shepherd's Pie

Like most potato-based dishes of mine, this is a boon to dieters—but I've never been on a "diet" in my life, and I love it! (I guess that's why I don't need to be "on a diet." When you love all these dishes, you won't, either.) The contrasting textures of the creamy mashed potatoes and the grainy millet, with the tasty vegetable layer in between, make an aesthetically pleasing "pie."

1/2 lb. fresh mushrooms, cleaned and minced
1 large or 2 medium onions, minced
2 medium to large carrots, peeled and minced
10-oz. package frozen cauliflower (can be allowed to thaw if time permits, but not necessary), or equivalent fresh cauliflower washed and chopped
1 c. uncooked millet
2 lbs. potatoes

White pepper
Onion powder
Garlic powder
Soy sauce (optional)
Parsley flakes

Prepare all vegetables. Start millet simmering as per directions on pages 17, 18. Start water boiling for potatoes. Scrub and peel potatoes and cut into large chunks. Cook as per directions for mashed potatoes on page 15.

Now that potatoes are simmering and millet has a good head start, cook veggies in skillet over moderate heat, stirring frequently. Add spices, except parsley, to taste. Cover and continue to stir and to taste for seasonings; as cauliflower thaws (if applicable) break it up into smaller chunks with edge of plastic spatula. (If that doesn't work, remove from pan and cut with knife, but don't let anyone see.) If veggies finish before millet, turn off heat and keep warm in tightly covered pan.

As soon as millet is done, spread it over bottom of large, deep glass or ceramic casserole, packing it slightly with back of spoon to make a good "crust." Add veggies and smooth over top, packing very slightly. By this time potatoes should be done—after a little practice, it's amazing how well the timing can work out. Drain and mash them with generous amounts of black and white pepper and parsley flakes. Add a little hot tap water, if needed, so they achieve a smooth, spreadable consistency. Spoon over veggies and spread with a knife or cake froster (What! you still own one of those? Shame!), swirling the top a little. Make sure potatoes "seal" all over dish to edge. Sprinkle additional black and white pepper over top.

Place dish under broiler with top of potatoes about 4-5 inches from heat. Broil 10-15 minutes until top of dish is a nice deep brown, turning dish occasionally if your broiler broils unevenly as mine does.

Note: If you've had a real glitch in your timing and the millet and veggies have gotten stone cold, a microwave can rescue you. Cook covered on about 3/4 power for 5-10 minutes, turning once, until reasonably hot, then let the broiler finish the job. Or bake, covered, 20-30 minutes in 350° oven before broiling—but this does tend to dry out the dish.

To serve: Cut into six, eight, or nine pieces, using sharp knife to cut through browned crust. Remove carefully, using two spatulas (spatulae?), and have a contest to see who can get it onto the plate in the neatest pie condition, with layers straight and together. Refrigerate and reheat leftovers in same manner as for potatoes nicoise (page 42). Note: If you have a lot left over, you can refrigerate it in the same casserole dish—I hate to wash dishes, especially unnecessarily. (That wasn't recommended for potatoes nicoise because they were cooked in a bulky electric skillet or fry pan, silly! If you're wondering why they weren't microwaved, it's because the bottom layer of potatoes browns so beautifully and deliciously—hadn't you noticed?) Accompany, if desired, with cooked broccoli, Brussels sprouts, or asparagus.

Yield: Serves 2-4.

PER 1/4 RECIPE

Protein 12g
Carbohydrates 48g
Fat 1.8g
Calories ....332(!)
Fat by Calories............................4.9%

Black Beans and Rice

I almost (*almost!*) feel guilty for including in a cookbook something which takes so little cooking and can actually consist of little more than opening a can. But I grew to love this dish during my years in Miami, where it is a staple in that city's many Cuban restaurants. I wouldn't have known about it otherwise, and if you don't have Cuban restaurants in your town, you may not know about it either, unless I tell you. So I shall. And it *is* nice to have a few "quickie" recipes available when you're too rushed or too tired for something that requires more extensive preparation.

Don't be bashful about loading on the raw onions—they're the star of the dish in terms of taste; there are no other seasonings to dim their luster! They also provide crunch not found in their cooked counterparts who populate the rest of this book. Nevertheless, it still might be wise not to eat this before your blind date. (Then again, it might, for protection!)

2 cups raw brown rice
1 16-oz. can black beans, undrained, or
    2 cups cooked-from-scratch (save
    cooking broth)
1 medium to large onion

Start rice cooking as per directions on page 27. Now go do something else for an hour. (See, I told you it was convenient!) Or use leftover cooked rice, if you have enough, for a really great use of same and an ultra-quick dinner.

When rice is done, start beans simmering over low heat in covered pot, in their packing or cooking liquid, and start your chosen veggie(s) in microwave or on stovetop, as desired. (Rice is supposed to sit a few minutes anyway, remember?) Meanwhile, peel and chop onion. Stir veggies and beans as required until done. And you're done!

To serve: Portion rice out on plates. Spoon beans over top, including some juice. Serve onions in bowl and allow each diner to top all with desired amount of onions. Remind diners that since everyone is eating raw onions, everyone can eat them.

With simple fare such as this, I often serve two or even three vegetables on the side. Bright green makes a good highlight against the black-and-white main dish, and cooked spinach seems to have a natural affinity for the beans and rice. Other favorites are cooked broccoli, Brussels sprouts, and asparagus. Include your favorites, but skip the white stuff, such as cauliflower, and other legumes such as peas or lima beans.

Store leftovers either separately, which allows you to use the rice for something else if such need comes up first, or with beans and rice mixed together. Add a little water and reheat in microwave or over low heat in saucepan; then sprinkle raw onions on top. (Yes, you can save any leftover onions from dinner, but wrap them very tightly in plastic wrap or bags *and* in aluminum foil, or your whole refrigerator will smell like onions.)

Yield: Serves 2-4.

PER 1/4 RECIPE

Protein... 15g
Carbohydrates 89g
Fat..2.1g
Calories.. 440
Fat by Calories 4.3%

Gumbo

I know that Louisiana is in America, but this recipe wasn't included under American foods because the distinctive nature of Creole cooking has its roots in the battles between the Spanish and the French over control of that state, and the attendant mixture of cuisines (and other things).

Wherever they come from, this dish and its variation with pasta are good. Vary the traditional hot pepper spicing to your taste; I use crushed red pepper flakes, rather than bottled hot pepper sauces, to avoid the salt in the latter, as well as to give a fresher taste.

Okra is another one of those vegetables, like squash or Brussels sprouts, that one isn't supposed to like. It doesn't have much taste on its own, but to me that's an open invitation to use it in a spicy recipe such as this, where it will pick up and absorb a myriad of other flavors. Since I started using this recipe, okra has become one of my favorites.

1 medium to large onion
1 green bell pepper
1 32-oz. can tomatoes, undrained
1 lb. fresh or frozen okra (if frozen,
    buy the pre-cut, not whole)
1 tsp. basil
1 tbsp. parsley flakes
1 tbsp. crushed red pepper, or more to
    taste
2 c. raw brown rice

Start rice cooking as per recipe on page 27. Chop onion and cut green pepper into thin, bite-sized strips. Sauté both in a little water in 3-qt. or larger pot for about 5 minutes, covering if you like your peppers very tender. Add juice from tomatoes. Chop tomatoes and add. Add okra and seasonings. Simmer covered, stirring occasionally, for 15 minutes or more, until okra is thoroughly tender. Serve over hot cooked rice.

Yield: Serves 2-4. Note: Leftovers reheat marvelously in microwave or on stove; rice and veggies can be stored together.

Variation: Add 2-3 stalks celery, chopped, at start of cooking.

PER 1/4 RECIPE

Protein.. 11g
Carbohydrates............................. 89g
Fat..2.2g
Calories 413
Fat by Calories........................... 4.9%

Variation: Gumbo With Pasta and Beans

Substituting a roughly equivalent amount of pasta and beans makes not only a nontraditional gumbo, but a nontraditional use of pasta as well, for a change of pace from Italian-type dishes. It's also an easy, one-pot meal with a variety of flavors and textures.

To make this variation, omit the rice and add 1 can drained pinto or other beans and 6 ounces whole-wheat corkscrews, elbows, or other pasta to the finished gumbo mix, above. (You will need to use a much larger pot—at least 5 quarts—to have room for the pasta to boil.) Bring to a boil, stirring frequently, and expect the pasta to take much longer to cook than the package tells you. Its cooking will also thicken the dish considerably, so you may have to add extra hot tap water. Cook until done by taste test, and serve by itself. (You could cook the pasta separately and add to the gumbo, but this way the pasta absorbs the gumbo flavors as it cooks and lends its flavors to the gumbo.)

You may store leftovers in the original pot, if there is a lot, and reheat slowly, adding water if needed to thin. Or, for smaller amounts, store in bowls and microwave straight from the fridge.

Yield: Serves 2-4.

PER 1/4 RECIPE

Protein.. 18g
Carbohydrates............................. 71g
Fat..1.8g
Calories 359
Fat by Calories........................... 4.6%

Let us conclude our dinner tour of the vegetarian world with a visit to what will be, for most Americans, the most exotic region: the Middle East and India.

Chapter 8: Middle Eastern/Indian

Curry Favor With Curry Flavor!

This chapter was placed last among dinner menus because some of the dishes and ingredients will be less familiar to many readers. Since the whole idea of vegetarian cooking is a bit foreign to most of us, it perhaps stands to reason that the most exotic dishes will make the best use of this "strange" cuisine.

India has many states or entire regions which are vegetarian for religious reasons, abstaining not only from the proverbial sacred cow but from poultry and fish as well. Therefore, most Indian restaurants offer a large selection of vegetarian dishes. Many vegetarian Indian specialties contain cheese or a similar curd-type product; virtually all are cooked in clarified butter, known as *ghee*. So whenever my travels take me to an Indian restaurant, I find that no matter how carefully I order, I end up doing funny things to my digestive tract, which is not accustomed either to fat or to animal products.

Middle Eastern restaurants, such as Persian, Moroccan, and Tunisian, are not as consciously vegetarian-oriented. Because of Persia's proximity to India and the shared beliefs of some of its populace, the cuisine of Persia (Iran) usually includes a few vegetable dishes on the menu, especially egg-plant. Here, though, the drawback is not butter, but olive oil—tons of the stuff, and eggplant soaks it up like a sponge. The Moroccan and Tunisian menus I have perused were heavily chicken-oriented, with other meat and fish dishes, and perhaps one vegetable dish, such as a cold tabouli salad, appearing to be an afterthought.

All is not lost, however. I recently discovered a tremendous serendipity in the form of Ethiopian restaurants. (I know, I know. Ethiopia is in Africa, but so is Egypt, and everyone calls Egypt part of the Middle East.) Virtually half the menu in many Ethiopian restaurants is vegetarian: using lentils, collards, bulgur wheat, and *injera*, a shortening-free bread made by fermentation. These ingredients are imaginatively spiced, scooped up with the bread, and deposited eagerly (and frequently, I might add) in one's oral cavity.

Unfortunately, I am afraid that there may not be a lot of Ethiopian restaurants in communities less multiethnic than Los Angeles. I am informed, for example, that there exists not a single Ethiopian restaurant in the entire city of Idaho Falls, Idaho. Until this sad situation is remedied, those of you who live in the hinterlands will have to console yourselves with the delightful knowledge that a vast assortment of Indian and Middle Eastern delicacies can be prepared using our no-fat vegetarian methods. Here are some ideas and recipes to get you started.

About Bulgur

Bulgur is parboiled, dried, cracked whole wheat. It is less refined than whole-wheat flour, yet it cooks quickly due to having been parboiled and cracked. It is available in health-food stores and some supermarkets. Bulgur comes in the form of grains, a little smaller than rice; if your store offers a selection of grinds, choose the coarsest.

Bulgur has got to be the easiest of all grains to prepare. Bring it to a boil with three parts water (or pour boiling water over it), shut off heat, cover tightly, and let sit 10 minutes. That's it! Drain it through a cheesecloth or very thin towel (not all of the water will be absorbed), squeezing well to remove excess moisture. The nutty, wheaty taste is a delight—use your imagination and serve it anywhere any other grain is called for, or use it as a side dish or base for a quick, hot, nourishing lunch. My favorite use for bulgur, however, is in couscous. Note: If you are serving bulgur directly from the stove, rather than in a recipe which calls for further cooking, add another 10-15 minutes to the steaming time, using a little heat, if necessary, until tender.

Couscous

Couscous has two meanings. It refers to a grain product common in Middle Eastern cooking, consisting of small granules of semolina flour, much like ground-up (white) spaghetti. It also refers to a dish made with this grain and assorted vegetables, of which there are many varied recipes. I prefer to make my couscous casserole with whole-grain bulgur rather than the refined flour used in the commercial couscous product; it has much more flavor, in addition to the whole-grain health advantages.

The cold relish served on the side provides not only the usual contrasts for which I strive in most of my creations—taste, texture, and color—but temperature contrast, as well. There is no duplication in the fact that tomatoes thereby appear twice in this dish; the hot and cold portions lend completely different effects to the finished product.

4 1/2 c. water
1 1/2 c. bulgur
2 medium to large onions
2 large or 3 medium carrots
1 lb. yellow summer squash
    (crookneck)
1 lb. fresh cauliflower (about 3/4
    medium or 2/3 large head)
1 1/2 lb. ripe tomatoes

Relish:
1 1/2 lb. ripe tomatoes (2 large or 3
    medium)
2-3 cloves garlic, minced
2 large or 3 medium scallions (or
    green onions), minus leafy tops,
    minced
2 tbsp. parsley flakes
1 tsp. cumin
1 tsp. crushed red pepper flakes, more
    or less to taste

Note: If convenient last-minute preparation is a factor, relish can be made ahead of time and refrigerated, tightly wrapped, for several hours or days.

Bring water to boil in 2-quart saucepan. Plunge tomatoes (for relish) into water for 8-12 seconds, depending on size; then remove and place under cold running water (to make them easy to peel). When water resumes boiling, add bulgur, stir, shut off heat, cover tightly, and allow to steam for 10 minutes.

Meanwhile, quarter onions (or eighth if large), peel carrots and cut into 2-inch spears, cut squash into large cubes, and break or cut cauliflower into florets. If bulgur isn't done yet (you *are* fast), start on relish.

When bulgur is done and drained, place on bottom of large, deep casserole. Layer or assort veggies on top of bulgur. Cover and microwave for 30 minutes on 80 percent power ("Reheat"), rotating dish once, or bake in 350° oven 30-45 minutes, until vegetables are tender.

While casserole cooks, peel, core, and chop tomatoes finely for relish. Add remaining ingredients and stir well in serving bowl. Let stand until ready to use, stirring one more time after a while.

Chop remaining (unpeeled) tomatoes coarsely. When casserole is within 5-10 minutes of completion, place tomatoes in 2-quart saucepan (you can use the one in which the bulgur was cooked—I *really* hate to wash dishes!) and simmer covered over low heat, stirring occasionally, until just tender. Do not overcook—you do not want stewed tomatoes.

To serve: Scoop portions of casserole onto plates, making sure to get top-to-bottom layers. (The first portion, as usual, is the hardest with which to achieve this.) Spoon hot tomatoes over top; then allow diners to spoon cold relish, to taste, into gaps in hot tomato covering. (Hey, you still don't want tomatoes on top of tomatoes, do you? This way you get alternate effects in the same, or alternate, bites.)

Leftovers are best refrigerated with all three components separate—casserole, hot tomatoes, and relish, although if you are pinched for space (as, for example, in brown-bagging), hot tomatoes could be mixed in with casserole. Reheat in microwave (best) or, with a little water, on stovetop, and serve as above, with relish straight from the refrigerator or at room temperature.

Yield: Serves 2-4.

PER 1/4 CASSEROLE

Protein	14g
Carbohydrates	76g
Fat	1.9g
Calories	348
Fat by Calories	4.9%

Another very satisfying and filling "diet" dish!

Rice Pilaf

Pilaf (or pilau) refers to any preparation of spiced rice; as a restaurant main dish, it is usually made with lamb or other meat or fish. It is often served in meatless versions as a side dish or as a base for other meat or vegetable preparations. Our version is tasty enough to serve as a main dish, with your favorite green vegetables on the side. You could also use it as a base for any other dish which is served on a bed of grain, such as stuffed grape leaves (page 53). Be sure to try some of the suggested variations too.

2 medium onions, finely chopped
2-4 cloves garlic, crushed
2 c. uncooked brown rice
**4 c. water or vegetable stock (you
    could use vegetable bouillon
    cubes, but they're awfully salty)**
Pinch crumbled saffron
2 tbsp. parsley flakes
1/2 tsp. cumin
1/2 tsp. coriander
**1/2 tsp. cinnamon, or more for those
    with a sweet tooth**
3 whole bay leaves

Note: Saffron is available at gourmet and specialty shops and some supermarkets. It is incredibly expensive—much more so than that no-no marijuana, according to what I read in the newspapers—but, in my opinion, absolutely essential to the character of the dish. Fortunately, it takes very little and is very light—I purchased a small tube which will be enough for three or four recipes.

Sauté onions and garlic in a bit of water in a 3-quart or larger saucepan until tender. Add rice and continue to cook, stirring almost constantly and adding a little water as needed, so onions brown a bit and rice absorbs flavors. Add remaining ingredients, bring to a boil, stir, reduce heat, cover tightly, and simmer undisturbed over very low heat for 1-1 1/2 hours or until almost all liquid is absorbed. Remove from heat, place towel under lid and recover, and keep warm for 5-10 minutes to absorb additional excess liquid. Serve immediately.

Serving suggestions: Broccoli, spinach, asparagus, Brussels sprouts, or broiled tomatoes (page 81) make good accompaniments. Refrigerate leftovers in original pot and reheat on stove, adding a little water, or refrigerate in microwavable container or bowls, heat in microwave, and serve directly from oven.

Yield: Serves 2-4.

PER 1/4 RECIPE

Protein	6g
Carbohydrates	69g
Fat	1.6g
Calories	319
Fat by Calories	4.6%

Add several cooked veggies, and you still have a very "calorie-cheap" dish!

Variations: For color as well as texture and flavor appeal, add a few frozen peas, very finely chopped carrot, and/or perhaps a touch of pimento, minced. Or substitute other grains, especially bulgur or millet, reducing the cooking time in these cases to about 30-40 minutes, and adjusting the water accordingly, to 6 cups if using 2 cups of grain. You can also make a very colorful pilaf by using 1 cup of bulgur and 1 cup of rice, and 5 cups of liquid.

For lentil pilaf, substitute 1/2 cup lentils (or split red or yellow peas) for 1/2 cup rice.

49

For a tangier flavor, which is especially recommended with the wheat (bulgur) and lentil pilafs, omit cinnamon and add 1 finely minced carrot and 1 teaspoon each onion powder and garlic powder. (This changes Nutritional Data to: 8/66/1.5 grams, respectively; calories remain about the same; 4.2% fat.)

About Eggplant

When someone wants a metaphor for the unappetizing or wants to make a joke about distasteful vegetables, eggplant is probably chosen more often than any other vegetable, with the possible exception of Brussels sprouts. It is hard to understand why this versatile, beautiful purple vegetable has been so maligned, until we take a look at what is usually done to it. Even so authoritative a source as *Joy of Cooking*, the veritable bible of conventional cookery, admonishes us to sprinkle the eggplant slices with salt, stack heavy weights on them between absorbent paper, and rub the slices with lemon juice. These measures are variously prescribed, according to their various advocates, to draw out excess water, to eliminate "bitter" juices, and/or to prevent discoloration.

When I became more familiar with vegetables (as a result of eating nothing else!) and realized that bitterness is generally a result of overcooking (or over-ripe vegetables, especially in Brussels sprouts, which are quite sweet when fresh), I gained the confidence simply to slice an eggplant and use it. I found, really not too much to my surprise, that properly cooked eggplant is not at all bitter, that the wateriness (which is not that much higher than most vegetables, which are mostly water, anyway) will cook off, and is even an asset in no-oil, nonstick cooking, and that if you use it immediately, instead of letting it sit around with dinner plates or books on it for half an hour or so, it won't have time to discolor. It is time to explode the eggplant-pretreatment myth once and for all, and I am proud to be the one to do so.

I do admit, however, that if one is accustomed to burying one's vegetables under butter, cheese, or sugar the rather mild taste of eggplant may seem bland, or even bitter, by comparison. Those who have read this far, however, will know by now that to the creative vegetarian, bland, absorbent vegetables are an open invitation to match with contrasting textures and bold spices. This is done in the following recipes for baked stuffed eggplant and eggplant with millet pilaf, and earlier in this book the eggplant was shredded and blended with other ingredients beyond recognition, as in shamburgers or sausage subs. First, though, I am going to give a recipe for plain, naked eggplant, absolutely free of adornments, partly to show that it can be done (and to show what eggplant *should* taste like), but mostly because it's a delicious side dish, with anything from shamburgers to stuffed grape leaves. In fact, we like it so much we use it as a main dish, with several green vegetables on the side, but be warned: the high fiber and water content does make it very filling on an awfully small number of calories, so you may find you're hungry later if you haven't had some bread or some such with it.

You want it thoroughly done—underdone eggplant is tough and fibrous—and you want it nicely browned for taste, but don't let the peel get too crisp. If you do it right, it will actually taste, not bitter, but downright *sweet*. Don't believe me? Try it.

Broiled Eggplant

Slice any number of eggplants into one-half to three-quarter-inch slabs, discarding stems. (Do not peel.) Spray nonstick baking sheet with nonstick vegetable spray. (Use multiple trays for large quantities, broiling and serving in shifts as you whisk one tray out and shoot another in.) Put slices on tray and broil on top rack until nicely browned, about 5-10 minutes. (If your broiler is not too even, you may have to move them around on the tray from time to time. Or serve the done ones first while the remainder finish cooking—that gives a continuous supply of fresh, hot slices, albeit at the inconvenience of jumping up and down during dinner.) Turn and broil until second side is brown also. Serve immediately. Keep any extra servings warm in warm oven, with broiler off; if they will have to wait a long time, cover with foil, although this tends to make them mushier. Refrigerate leftovers, tightly wrapped, and reheat in microwave, under broiler, or baked in sealed aluminum foil. (See note above on mushiness.)

Yield: As a side dish, allow 1 pound per person; as a main dish (see note above and ridiculously low calorie count below) allow 2-3 pounds per person.

PER POUND

Protein	4g
Carbohydrates	21g
Fat	0.7g
Calories	92
Fat by Calories	6.8%

Variations: Now that you've finally seen what eggplant itself tastes like, you can go ahead and try sprinkling black pepper and/or garlic powder on it before broiling, and see which of the three you like best.

Baked Stuffed Eggplant

Now we get to the fancier stuff. Different flavors, textures, and spices make this a true gourmet treat, yet eggplant's high-fiber, low-calorie qualities keep it in the realm of the dieter's dream.

2 large or 3 medium eggplants; total about 3 lbs.
1 large onion
2-4 cloves garlic, crushed
1 lb. ripe tomatoes
1 tbsp. oregano
3 tbsp. parsley flakes
1 tsp. cinnamon, plus additional for garnish
1 c. tightly packed crumbs from cornbread (page 78)

Pierce whole eggplants several times with a fork. Microwave about 10 minutes on full power, turning and rotating once, or bake on sheet in 350° oven about 30 minutes, until not quite done. Meanwhile, chop onion, core and chop tomatoes into half-inch cubes and, if microwaving, start garlic and onions sautéing in electric or other skillet over medium heat. (If baking, wait until eggplants are almost done.)

When eggplants are ready, remove from oven and cut in half lengthwise. Add tomato to skillet. Run paring knife around inside of each eggplant half, leaving a quarter to half-inch and being careful not to pierce the shell. (This will be hard to avoid if they are too done.) Scoop out insides with a spoon, and an occasional assist from a knife, if necessary; chop pulp and add to skillet along with seasonings. Cook, covered, about five minutes, stirring frequently; reduce heat if necessary to avoid sticking. Preheat oven to 375°. (For once, do not use microwave.) Crumble cornbread, add to mixture, stir, and remove from heat.

Place eggplant halves, open side up, in one or two glass casserole or baking dishes, as needed. (You may spray them with a non-stick spray for easier cleanup.) Fill each half with cooked mixture, dividing evenly; heap up slightly as required, but do not pack. Sprinkle additional cinnamon to taste over tops. Bake 40 minutes; cornbread crumbs should be starting to brown. Serve immediately.

Serving suggestions: In my experience, nothing seems to go as well with this dish as cooked spinach, fresh or frozen.

Variation: If good, ripe tomatoes aren't available, canned tomatoes make an acceptable, though less desirable substitute. I'd certainly rather use them than the pink plastic ones (produced by "gassing" tomatoes picked green for shipment) which some stores sell.

Yield: Serves 2. As noted, this is a very "lean" dinner, unless bread is added.

PER 1/2 RECIPE

Protein	14g
Carbohydrates	80g
Fat	2.1g
Calories	361
Fat by Calories	5.2%

Eggplant/Millet Pilaf

This pilaf recipe is milder than the one called for as a variation of rice pilaf (page 49), because it is topped with eggplant which has been marinated and baked in a flavorful sauce of its own (in which we finally use lemon without eggplant, though without the salt, of course!). The result is still fairly mild (by my standards, anyway), so I like to serve this on a night which is between two nights of spicy recipes, such as, say, tostadas and chow mein.

2 medium eggplants
4 tbsp. water
1 lemon or lime, juiced
3 cloves garlic, crushed
1 tsp. soy sauce (if on salt-free diet, use garlic and onion powder instead)

Pilaf:
1 large onion
3-5 cloves garlic, crushed
1 1/2 c. raw millet
1 tsp. ground coriander
6 whole cloves
4 1/2 c. boiling water

Pierce whole eggplants with a fork. Microwave on full power 10 minutes, turning and rotating once, or bake in 350° oven on sheet 30 minutes, until just barely done. (Slightly underdone is OK—they will cook some more later.) Slice thickly, three-quarters to an inch, and place in layers in shallow glass baking dish. Mix remaining marinade ingredients and pour over eggplant. Start preheating oven, if not already used, to 350°.

Chop onion finely. Sauté it and the garlic for a few minutes in a 3-quart or larger saucepan, covered, over moderate heat. Add the millet and coriander and sauté for another 3 minutes or so, stirring frequently and adding a bit of water as needed to prevent sticking. Add cloves and boiling water, turn heat up to high, and bring to a boil, stirring occasionally. Reduce heat, cover, and simmer undisturbed over very low heat for 20-25 minutes, or until millet is tender and water is absorbed. After covering the millet, place eggplant dish in oven and bake, covered, until millet is done.

To serve: Spoon millet onto plates, flatten slightly with back of spoon, and cover millet "bed" with eggplant slices. Diners cut eggplant and eat with millet in each bite. Add a crisp green vegetable, such as broccoli.

Leftovers may be stored together in tightly wrapped casserole or bowl and reheated in microwave, or, awkwardly, over low heat in tightly covered saucepan with a little water.

Variation: Add a little black and/or white pepper to the marinade, or sprinkle over finished eggplant slices.

Yield: Serves 2-3, or a lean 4, if not stretched with a filling accompaniment. (You could also stretch by increasing millet to 2 cups and water to 6 cups, especially if your eggplants are very large.)

PER 1/4 RECIPE

Protein..9g
Carbohydrates............................ 60g
Fat...2.2g
Calories......................................268
Fat by Calories 7.5%

You now have enough ammunition to refute the next person who makes a disparaging remark about eggplant. We therefore turn our attention to other Mideastern staples (though eggplant could yet sneak in somewhere again!).

Curried Vegetables

Curry is to Indian cooking what chow mein is to Chinese—a generic term for a dish with a wide range of spices and ingredients, for which there are as many recipes as chefs. It's easy to make without the standard Indian clarified butter, and a tasty change from just about anything else!

My first encounter with curry—and last, for many years—was some tasteless, thick yellow glop, served over chicken, probably in a school cafeteria. I am now told that this American conception of curry is the result of mistaken impressions by the British during their tenure there. If you've suffered the same indignity, this recipe will set the record straight, deliciously.

1 large or 2 medium eggplants
2 cloves garlic, crushed
1 tsp. tumeric
1 tsp. cumin
1/4 tsp. or more cayenne, to taste
2 tsp. ground coriander
1 large or 2 medium potatoes, unpeeled
1/2 package frozen green beans
1 small or 1/2 large cauliflower
1 jalapeño pepper
1 tsp. ginger
1 lb. ripe tomatoes
2 c. raw brown rice

Pierce eggplant with a fork and microwave on full power for 3 minutes, or boil (without piercing) for 5 minutes. Remove and let cool. Start rice, as per directions on page 27.

Put spices in large skillet. Add just enough water to make a thin paste and cook over low heat for a few minutes, stirring frequently and adding more water as needed. Meanwhile, dice eggplants and potatoes. Add them to skillet, along with green beans. Break cauliflower into florets and add to skillet. Mince jalapeño and add. Core and chop tomatoes and add. Cover and simmer gently, stirring occasionally, for about 20 minutes, or until potatoes are thoroughly tender. Serve over hot cooked rice.

Yield: Serves 2-4. Leftovers may be refrigerated with rice and reheated in microwave, or in saucepan with a little water added.

Variations: 1 teaspoon ground cloves and/or 1 teaspoon ground cardamon seed to spice mixture.

PER 1/4 RECIPE

Protein	14g
Carbohydrates	102g
Fat	2.5g
Calories	468
Fat by Calories	4.7%

Stuffed Grape Leaves

A popular Middle Eastern dish, usually made with lamb and dripping with olive oil, which is often served cold as an appetizer as well as hot as a main dish (cold lamb fat and olive oil—ugh!). These fall into the category of dishes which require a lot of preparation time but long, undisturbed cooking time, so start assembling them about 2 1/2 hours ahead of dinner time (even 3 hours, until you get the hang of it), but figure on being able to do something else for most of the last 1 1/2 hours.

You should be able to find grape leaves at Middle Eastern grocery stores and general gourmet shops if they are not at your local supermarket, but I have had little trouble buying them in grocery stores in towns large and small.

1 16-oz. jar grape leaves
2 medium onions
2/3 c. raw brown rice
3 tbsp. parsley flakes
2 tbsp. dill weed
Dash cinnamon
2 1/2 c. hot water
1 1/2 c. raw millet

Remove grape leaves from jar carefully so as not to tear them. They will be bunched up. Soak them in very hot water for about 10 minutes, separating them as they loosen up, and drain on paper towels. Chop onions finely and mix with rice and spices in mixing bowl. Place a teaspoon or more of mixture on each leaf, shiny side down, according to size of leaf. Do not overfill—you want plenty of room to roll them up, and remember, the rice will swell as it cooks. Fold over sides, then roll up from bottom (wide part) to tip, again, not super-tightly.

Place leaves seam-side down in large, flat-bottomed kettle (4-5 quart). Add 2 1/2 cups hot water. Cover leaves with a heavy plate to weigh them down. Cover pot and simmer 1 1/2 hours. When leaves are 1/2 hour from being done, cook millet as per directions on page 17.

To serve: Make a bed of millet on each plate. Carefully remove grape leaves from pot with a plastic spoon (less chance of tearing them than with a metal spoon) and lay seam-side down on millet. Using a squeeze-bulb type baster (Oops!—you threw it out when you quit eating meat? Use a spoon.), shlurp up some of the yummy broth from the bottom of the pot and squirt it over the leaves and millet. Diners cut leaves into bite-sized pieces (it takes a sharp knife, like a st**k knife) and eat with a forkful of millet.

For beautiful color, and because the acidity complements the tanginess of the spiced leaves, the sole and perfect accompaniment is broiled tomatoes (page 81).

Refrigerate leftover leaves and millet together and reheat in microwave (the leaf juices will run into the millet, which absorbs them so nicely, as we've pointed out before), or, less desirably, steam them in saucepan with a little water over low heat.

Yield: Serves 2-4; may be bulked up by cooking 2 cups of millet instead of 1 1/2.

Nutritional data note: I have been unable to find a brand of grape leaves which carries nutritional statistics on its label, and they are not in my otherwise encyclopedic *Composition of Foods* handbook. Because they look to me to be reasonably similar in character to fresh spinach leaves, I have used the data for fresh spinach in order to construct estimated values. It should be fairly close; if I am wrong in this, the difference should not prove harmful to you, much less fatal. (Most of the calories, carbs, etc., are in the rice and millet, anyway.)

PER 1/4 RECIPE

Protein 11g
Carbohydrates............................. 75g
Fat 2.6g
Calories......................................342
Fat by Calories...............................7%

Variation: Instead of serving leaves over millet, serve over bulgur, rice (a good use for leftover rice), or rice pilaf, as suggested on page 49.

Stuffed Cabbage

One form or another of stuffed cabbage seems to show up in many European and Asian cuisines—Polish, Hungarian, kosher, etc. It's certainly understandable, for this versatile vegetable will complement—and, even more important, will hold—just about whatever stuffing is called for by the local gastronomy. I've included it here because I use bulgur, which is Middle Eastern in character, as a principal stuffing ingredient. It also seems appropriate to close out our dinner recipes (but not the book!) with the most elaborate preparation, resulting in the creation of a crowning glory. Start this one at 2:00 p.m. if you want to eat at 7:00 p.m. until you've done it once (it's really a two-person job). You will, however, have 2 1/2 hours of undisturbed time before dinner. And the result *is* artistically beautiful—a whole cabbage head, miraculously reformed, which, when cut, reveals layers as pretty as a cake—and it makes plenty, for company or a second night's dinner. It's worth the effort, especially on a cold winter day when the heat from the oven feels so good!

Julia Child once did a stuffed cabbage with bulgur. She had the right idea, but she used eggs, cheese, and butter. You can take French chefs out of France, but you can't take the French out of their cooking. I can, though, and while I dare not (yet?) style myself the Julia Child of vegetarianism, I do humbly suggest that if dear Julia tried this delicious, low-calorie dish, she'd become a mere wisp of a girl, or at least have more room for all those desserts!

Note: I strongly advise that you do all vegetable preparations in advance, before starting any cooking, or you'll go crazy. Also note that you have to start a whole day ahead of time to freeze the cabbage. This is not your basic think-I'll-run-to-the-store-and-get-something-for-dinner, last-minute dish.

1 3 lb. cabbage, plus 6 more large leaves
3 large or 6 medium onions: 1/3 sliced, 1/3 chopped, 1/3 minced
2 large or 4 small carrots; 1/2 chopped, 1/2 sliced
2 medium celery ribs, diced
1 lb. fresh mushrooms, cleaned and minced
2 c. bulgur
1 30-oz. can tomato purée
At various times: thyme, mint, lemon juice, cloves, bay leaves, garlic powder, onion powder, parsley flakes, basil, marjoram, oregano.

Core cabbage head very deeply, for easy future leaf removal. Freeze, tightly wrapped in plastic wrap, overnight (or longer, if desired). Meanwhile, beg, borrow, or steal the largest stainless-steel mixing bowl you can find. I've got one that holds 4 quarts and is 8 1/2" in diameter, and it does very nicely.

On D-day (C-day?), drop cabbage head into boiling water. Gently separate leaves as you are able, letting each stay in the water an extra minute or so to soften, then plunge into cold water and drain. Blanch, cool, and drain the extra leaves also. Now put them all someplace out of the way, such as the guest bathroom.

Cook bulgur in 3-quart saucepan as per directions on page 47, but for only 5 minutes. In the meantime, water-sauté the *chopped* onions, carrots, and the celery for a few minutes. When the bulgur is cooked, add the veggies and mix into this the mint, and lemon juice, generously. Remove from heat and from harm's way.

Water-sauté the mushrooms and *minced* onions in a large skillet or saucepan with thyme and black pepper until both are tender, about 5-8 minutes. Reserve. Also save any juice from the skillet.

Line the bottom of your big bowl with the *sliced* onions and carrots. You are now ready to begin the fun of reassembling your cabbage, thereby outdoing the king's horses and men in their attempt to reassemble Humpty Dumpty. Pretend you are playing with papier-maché.

Put the largest cabbage leaves (not the 6 extra) in the bottom and sides of the bowl, stem side up. Add a layer of bulgur mixture. Add a layer of leaves. Add a layer of mushroom mixture; add leaves. Repeat, alternating the different stuffings with leaves, ending with leaves. Preheat oven to 400°.

Pour the mushroom broth you presumably saved over the cabbage and add enough hot water to almost cover it. Throw in a couple of bay leaves and 4 cloves. Spray a sheet of aluminum foil with nonstick vegetable spray and cover cabbage tightly, wrapping over bowl. Bake 2 1/2 hours.

Place tomato purée in saucepan and season well with garlic powder, onion powder, parsley flakes, basil, marjoram, a bay leaf, and oregano (much less oregano than for, say, spaghetti sauce—you don't want this to be sweet). Simmer for at least 1/2 hour. You may prepare the sauce so it finishes when the cabbage does, or do it now and let it sit (or keep simmering if you *really* trust your stove or slow cooker). Or you might prefer to do it ahead of time, even on a previous day, then to refrigerate and reheat. The baking time should give you time to clean up the mess, but don't bother to wash the mushroom skillet.

To serve: This is really a two-person job. Fold back part of the foil and pour the liquid into the skillet in which you cooked the mushrooms (or any other skillet, if need be). Boil liquid down to about 1/3 cup and add it to the (reheated, if applicable) tomato sauce. Now one person holds a large serving plate or tray to the mouth of the bowl (remove the foil first!) while the other, using gloves or

potholder, attempts to invert the *heavy* bowl onto the plate. (See why it's a good thing you drained it well?)

Still with me? Nothing broken? No cabbage on the floor? Good, it's all easy from here. Cover the cabbage with the 6 extra leaves and allow the heat from the cabbage to warm them for a minute. With a very sharp knife, cut out serving wedges—sixths or eighths—from cabbage. With a spatula or cake server, and the help and guidance of the knife, carefully remove wedges to dinner plates, either standing up, if wide and thick enough, or lying on their sides, like a wedge of cake. Allow everyone to ooh and aah over the pretty layer effect; then spoon hot tomato sauce over all. Cover remaining cabbage with the foil you threw away a minute ago; the hot tomato sauce will make seconds adequately hot. Diners should cut servings with a sharp knife, as usual, trying to get some of each layer in each bite.

Wrap leftovers tightly with plastic wrap and/or foil on plate and refrigerate, with sauce separate. Reheat in microwave on 1/2 power, rotating frequently, and top with separately-reheated sauce; or cover with sauce, add a bit of water, and reheat over low heat in tightly-covered saucepan.

Variations: Each time you make this, vary who does the dishes.

Yield: Serves 3-6. Accompaniments would be an insult to your artwork.

PER 1/6 RECIPE

Protein	13g
Carbohydrates	73g
Fat	1.8g
Calories	331
Fat by Calories	4.8%

Note: If after eating all the cabbage, you have any leftover sauce (I don't; I like mine heavy on the sauce), refrigerate or freeze it and throw it in your next batch of spaghetti or pizza sauce.

This concludes our breathtaking tour of vegetarian dinners from around the world. Don't go away yet, though; there are still oodles of side dish and luncheon ideas to explore! But first, how about dessert?

Chapter 9: Tasty, Healthful Dinners Get Their Just Desserts

We were having one of my favorites, baked stuffed eggplant. (Oh, well, they're *all* my favorites, or they wouldn't be in this book!) After a few bites I looked up at Ruth.

"Did you put sugar in this?" I asked, with facetious wariness.

"No," she replied. "I was going to ask you if *you* did."

"You made it," I pointed out.

"Yes, but maybe you snuck in and added the sugar when I wasn't looking."

We both knew that neither had done any such thing, but we were agreed that the dish was unusually sweet. I asked her if she had used any extra cinnamon, the only really sweet spice in the recipe, and she assured me she had not. Finally, after I had bitten into a chunk of onion, I realized what it was: the latest batch of onions purchased had been even sweeter than normal, and cooking had only amplified that fact. (We also agreed that it was *good!*)

A funny thing happens after you eliminate from your diet all forms of concentrated sugars, such as table sugar, honey, fructose, etc. (Actually, it's not so funny when you think about it.) You begin to taste sweetness in foods in which you couldn't taste it before, or as strongly, such as corn, squash, and yams, and even in foods which are not at all regarded as sweet by most people, such as onions, garlic, Brussels sprouts, and yes—even eggplant. You not only savor the high glucose content of a fresh carrot, you can actually feel the lift it gives

you as your blood sugar level zips right up (but doesn't come crashing down again, as it would with a candy bar). This makes carrots an excellent snack when you're feeling draggy-hungry in between meals.

Yes, most vegetables do contain various sugars (they need to store energy too, you know), but who could taste their relatively minor quantities, after a breakfast consisting of a cereal which contains more sugar than flour (covered with milk, which adds even more sugar), and a soft drink at lunch which has the equivalent of nine teaspoons of the stuff?

The point of all this (you knew there was a point, didn't you?) is that a low-sugar lifestyle eventually changes your dessert preferences too. If an onion tastes sweet, think how incredibly sweet a pear is going to taste! It may have been hard to believe that your sweet tooth would ever abate, much less go away, but then wasn't it hard to believe that you'd ever lose your taste for dead meat, after eating the stuff for twenty, forty, or sixty years?

I remember an experiment we did in my fourth-grade science class, to demonstrate how enzymes in saliva convert starches to sugars as the first step in digestion. We were given a salt-free cracker and told to chew it extremely well, not swallowing it, and letting our saliva dissolve it. There was one girl in the class who hated sugar (boy, did we think she was weird!—actually she was way ahead of her time), and after about a minute she ran to the sink and spat—she couldn't take the taste anymore. I've seen exactly the same reaction, in myself and others, when, for example, I've been somewhere where doughnuts were served, and, being curious after not having had one in a year or so, I've tried a bite. Blecch!—the concentrated impact of so much sugar hitting the tongue at once was as distasteful as it would be to most people to swallow a tablespoon of salt by itself. (The effect on the stomach of the little bit that got swallowed accidently was about the same too.)

The analogy with salt is pretty good. Heavy salters can barely taste anything which isn't buried in the stuff, while those who abstain find that they begin to notice other flavors, including the natural saltiness of foods such as celery, and if they do decide to use salt (such as, say, in soy sauce) a little goes a long way.

So it is with dessert. Fruits are naturally much higher in sugar than the vegetables and grains whose sweetness you are now capable of perceiving. As a result, a mere unadorned piece of fresh fruit makes an incredibly sweet way to end dinner, leaving a pleasant taste in the mouth (and canceling out some of that hot Mexican stuff) and a satisfied feeling in the tummy and brain. To attempt to enhance such a delight could be not only superfluous, but counterproductive. A really good mango, in season, is almost too sweet to bear. How could you do anything else to it, but chill it, peel it, and eat it?

Nevertheless, there are times when you wish a change, or perhaps something hot on a cold day, or maybe there is not a lot of good fresh fruit available at the moment for seasonal reasons. For these reasons, I present here a few things to do with items available year-round, which should provide the variation needed.

Broiled Oranges

All summer long, a cornucopia of fresh fruit pours through the grocery store—peaches, strawberries, mangoes, grapes, blueberries, watermelon, honeydew, cantaloupe, etc., which are so good, either by themselves or in combination, that one is faced with the donkey-between-two-bales-of-hay situation. Fortunately, just as the approach of winter starts to stem this tide, the stores start featuring oranges from California and Florida. When you get tired of them cold, here's a variation which is completely different in taste and texture.

Split the oranges in half crosswise, i.e. at right angles to the core. Section them with a grapefruit knife, leaving the sections in place. Dust the top surface very generously with cinnamon, virtually covering it. Broil on second-highest rack on a baking sheet covered with aluminum foil, for easy cleanup. (Crimp the edges of the foil up to catch any stray juices.) Cook until edges of peels start to blacken and juices are bubbling vigorously, about 10 minutes. You want them to be heated all the way through, not just the tops, so they will be different from cold oranges. The sections may even start to pop up out of the shells—that's OK. Serve immediately; eat sections with a spoon. Don't neglect to scrape the peels or turn them inside out to get every last luscious bite!

Baked Apples, Pears, or Peaches

Decent apples are usually available year-round, so these are a good item to have in the repertoire when other fruit pickings are scarce—and again, they're completely different from fresh apples. Peaches, on the other hand, are highly seasonal, with the really good ones seeming to appear in just a few months of the summer; the different varieties of pears, with different maturation dates, provide a much longer season. Nevertheless, as enjoyable as a good, fresh peach or pear is, try them this way, too; they get even sweeter when cooked—the juice of a really lush peach will start to caramelize from the cooking, producing a thick syrup when you cut into it.

One other important use of the cooking method is to rescue fruit which is underripe, not very juicy, or not sweet enough. If you buy a batch of peaches and the first few you eat lack flavor, cook the remainder, for the sweetening mentioned above. I've even had the experience of biting into a pear I thought was ripe, only to find that it was still quite hard and unflavorful. Whisk!—into the microwave it goes, to emerge as a different, tasty treat.

To bake fruit, place each whole fruit in a separate plastic food-storage bag, of the fold-over-top type. Fold in the top loosely, so the steam can escape, but not the juice. Microwave on about half power ("Bake" or "Simmer"), turning once, until juices bubble vigorously (the skin will pop a leak to allow this). This will take about 6 minutes for two medium-sized fruits; adjust time according to quantity and size of fruit. Remove from oven and allow to sit in bags for about 3-5 minutes, steaming in their own juices. Empty fruit onto serving plates, saving juice; split fruit in half and pour juice over it. Eat with knife and fork—it's HOT! (Sugars and fats hold heat much better than the grains and fibers which make up most of the rest of the foods used in this book.)

If, after serving, you find the fruit is not quite done in the middle, don't panic. Place it on a microwavable dish, if your serving plates are not, and cover tightly with plastic wrap, face up. Poke a hole in the wrap. Microwave a few additional minutes on same setting until done, allow to sit another minute or two, and serve.

To bake in oven (less desirable, if my opinion), place apples on foil-covered baking sheet; place peaches and pears on same but cover with additional foil and crimp edges to make a tight steamer. (The more impervious skin of apples retains their moisture without this.) Bake at 350° for 30-60 minutes, according to size, until done all the way through. Serve as above.

Variation: Sprinkle cinnamon on split fruit, and microwave as described above for undercooked fruit, or bake as specified, reducing allotted time by a third or so. The split method is especially appropriate for unusually large pieces of fruit which might boil off all their surface juices before the inside is done. It also rescues the situation I described in which you bite into a fresh pear, only to find that it's underripe. (If you try to cook it whole, too much juice will run out where you bit. The plastic wrap or foil helps seal that in, while the splitting reduces the total cooking time so there's less time for the juice to dry.)

Nutritional note: Virtually any fruit you choose to cook or eat will have about 50-90 calories for a medium-sized (about 5-6 ounce) fruit, virtually all of it from carbohydrate, with generally less than a gram each of protein and fat. (Excluding, of course, the infamous 88 percent-fat avocado.) Com- pare that to just about any other dessert, including your newspaper's or magazine's "low-calorie" dessert recipes. Those who count calories very strictly, however, should be aware that fruit can be a lot larger than that—I've bought apples, pears, and peaches that weighed the better part of a pound each, and I've had mangoes that weighed two pounds!

Apple Crisp

Do you miss your hot apple pies and cobblers on cold winter nights or holidays? (Or on August 19, for that matter?) Of course you do. Here's something even better, full of genuine apple flavor and "crunch" that is not smothered in a floury, fatty crust. And it's actually quicker to make!

This recipe and the next one are a bit fancier than the foregoing, and a bit higher in calories as well. They're ideal for celebrations and special occasions.

Begin by choosing any number of red delicious or other suitable baking apples, cored and sliced, but not peeled

For *each* medium apple, use:
1-2 tsp. lemon juice, according to how
    tart apples are
1/4 tsp. cinnamon
1/4 c. Nutty Rice cereal (see discussion
    under Variations)
1/8 c. Crispy Oats cereal
1/8 tsp. cinnamon
1 tsp. vanilla
2-3 tbsp. water

For 1-3 servings, place each apple, sliced, in individual baking dish; for 4 or more, may be made en masse in one large baking dish, multiplying ingredients accordingly.

Preheat oven to 425°. Mix apple slices with lemon juice and cinnamon. Mix cereals and additional cinnamon and sprinkle over top. Mix water and vanilla and sprinkle over cereal topping. Bake, uncovered, 25-30 minutes until top is crisp and apples are tender and juicy. Allow to stand a few minutes, then serve.

Cooled leftovers may be refrigerated in same container, tightly wrapped, and reheated in 350° oven, covered with foil, for 15 minutes or so. (For once, microwaving is less desirable, though feasible if in a hurry, for either initial cooking or reheating, due to the resulting lack of crispness in the topping.)

Yield: One apple, with toppings, per person.

PER MEDIUM APPLE

Protein 3g
Carbohydrates............................. 49g
Fat 2.3g
Calories..215
Fat by Calories............................9.6%

Variations: You may peel the apple, if you wish; I feel the skins lend extra texture and tart flavor.

Endless variations can be made in your choice of cereal toppings; the two listed are merely two I have tried and like. You may use only one cereal, of whatever type; again, I like the different tastes and textures in the same dish. Some suggestions, especially if you cannot find the two listed above: Grape Nuts, Shredded Wheat (broken up but not crushed), oat or amaranth flakes, Oatio's, Puffed Kashi (use a second, denser cereal with this one), and Oat Bran Crunch.

Note: If neither of the cereals used has any sweetener added (barley malt, fruit juice, etc.), you may wish to add 1 teaspoon of frozen apple juice concentrate per apple, depending on the sweetness of your apples.

Ice Dream

We've had a special treat for cold weather; now how about one for hot? This no-fat, no-sugar frozen dessert recipe lets all the fruit flavor come through, with about half the calories of even the lowest-fat ice milks and frozen yogurts.

Speaking of the latter, please don't fall into the Tofutti trap or eat any of the other imitation ice creams or yogurts made with tofu or soy beans. Reread page 5 on the fattiness of soybean products. Given the choice, you'd be better off with low-fat frozen yogurt, ice milk, or plain old soft-serve from the corner Dairy Queen. You'd be accepting a relatively small amount of cholesterol—about 25 milligrams per cup or less—in return for a major fat reduction. If your answer is, "But I don't want *any* cholesterol"

(or "I'm allergic to milk, or lactose"), well, why do you think I printed this recipe?

Using frozen bananas gives a thicker consistency, closer to ice cream, but is more awkward to process if you have a blender rather than a food processor. Fresh bananas produce a lighter texture, more like frozen mousse, sherbet, or pudding, and can also be done on the spur of the moment, if you haven't kept bananas in the freezer. (For easiest future handling, peel bananas and cut into chunks *before* freezing, wrapping tightly in plastic wrap or bag and aluminum foil.)

For each serving:
1 ripe medium banana, peeled and cut into chunks, fresh or frozen (see note above)
3/4 c. frozen, unsweetened strawberries
1 tsp. vanilla extract

Blend all ingredients in food processor or blender, stopping occasionally to stir, if using blender. (Move frozen chunks down towards blade.) When all are broken up thoroughly and well mixed, serve immediately. Do not freeze finished product or leftovers—due to the lack of fat, it will resemble an ice cube. Garnish with fresh strawberries, if desired.

PER SERVING

Protein..2g
Carbohydrates............................. 32g
Fat..0.7g
Calories..126
Fat by Calories............................4.7%

Variations: Use other frozen, unsweetened fruits, such as blueberries, raspberries, peaches, etc. Or add a tablespoon of carob powder, available at health-food stores, for a chocolate-strawberry flavor. (Want straight chocolate flavor? Omit the fruit altogether and use frozen bananas and carob, plus vanilla, adding a very small amount of ice water, if needed, for processability.)

This makes a great change of pace from fresh or hot fruit desserts and is most welcomed by taste buds and stomachs which are now rebelling against concentrated fat.

Chapter 10: How to Drive Your Co-Workers Wild: Lunches and Side Dishes

Lunch (which could be at 3:00 a.m. if you work the graveyard shift) basically divides into two categories: (A) You eat at home, or have cooking/reheating facilities, such as a microwave or hotplate, available at work, and (B) You do not. Category B also includes situations such as picnics, hikes, or days at the beach, in which you choose not to lug along cooking equipment or start a campfire. In either category, you can eat surprisingly well, and thereby drive down the stock of fast-food chains.

Let's take a look at situation A first, because that's the easiest and offers the most diversity. (Many of its ideas can also be adapted to B with the proper hardware.) The simplest thing to have for lunch is leftovers from last night's dinner. Storage and reheating instructions were given for most dinner recipes where applicable; if you have a hot plate or microwave at work but no refrigerator, pack well-chilled leftovers tightly in airtight containers, and take to work in one of those nifty insulated cold-storage lunch bags.

There is nothing quite like the sight (and smell) of you eating couscous or baked stuffed eggplant to do a number on your colleagues. First they'll inhale the aroma, light up and then ask, "What is it?" when they don't recognize it. Then you have the fun of watching their reaction when you tell them. If you're really nice, you can offer the more adventurous a taste and enjoy their letdown when they turn to their now pale-looking peanut-butter-and-jelly sandwich.

Nutritional note: If the leftovers contain concentrated-protein items, such as beans or lentils, it's probably best not to have them for lunch on a day when you will be having other high-protein items for dinner, lest you overload your poor system with too much protein.

You may find, however, as I do, that you rarely have leftovers. Most of the recipes serve 2-4, and my helpmate and I served as the very hungry 2 by which that was computed. Or you may have enough left over to make a complete second night's dinner. (Lucky, lazy you!) Do not despair or start packing the peanut butter and jelly. You are about to see proof that Nature loves us.

Corn on the Cob

If microwave ovens were totally useless for any other purpose, they would have justified their invention, and purchase, solely for what they do for fresh-picked corn. Without water to leach away flavor and juice, or coals to scorch it, the natural sugars in the corn create one of those almost-too-sweet-to-eat sensations—savor carefully, and you can taste a creamy, buttery flavor too. Who needs to add butter or salt? (This assumes, however, that you have access to good corn, picked fresh, rushed to your store and to you, and stored properly in the interim. Old or out-of-season corn is terrible.)

Many consider the chief virtue of a microwave oven to be its reheating ability. That is akin to saying that Robert Redford's most valuable asset is his skiing ability. It's certainly nice that it's there, but I didn't even mention reheating in the discussion of the microwave on page 10 because, although it's far better for the purpose than other methods in most cases, what it does for reheated foods pales beside what it does for fresh ones.

The best way to buy corn is in the husk—its own natural wrapping. No, you don't need to buy unhusked corn (or unzip the husk a bit, as so many rude shoppers do) to judge its quality. Look for large, well-shaped ears, with fat ends, which feel hefty in your hand, compared to others. Those which are skinny, have scrawny tips, or feel light, are apt to have skinny, scrawny kernels which are light on flavor too. Buy yellow corn, not white; it has not only more flavor but more Vitamin A also. By the same token, if you *can* see the kernels, the darker yellow, the better. If only partially- or totally-husked corn is available, use color as well as other methods to choose it.

To microwave corn: Place ears in oven as far apart as possible—for two ears, put at opposite sides of oven; for three, make a large triangle, for four, a square, etc. (Four is probably a good limit to do at one time.) Cook on full power for 2-5 minutes per ear, depending on size, power of your oven, and even on freshness of the corn. Halfway through, turn each ear end for end, roll it 180°, and move the triangle or square around, or exchange places if doing two ears. This helps to assure even cooking, else you may find some kernels done and some not. Until you have enough experience with your oven and different-sized ears, check doneness by opening the husk a little and looking for kernels which are much darker than when raw, and uniformly so. Odor (aah!) and feel are also good guides; if still in doubt, take a *careful* bite, or kiss the roof of your mouth good-bye. If not done, rezip by unhusking completely and roll in a paper towel.

When done, husk carefully (I find a paper towel in each hand protects against burns) and allow corn to cool for a few minutes before attempting to eat it. Store second- or third-serving ears, unhusked, back in the oven or otherwise protected from drafts, to keep warm, but note that some cooking will continue to take place. Tip: Stop cooking when smallest ears are done, and eat them first; the larger ones will be done by the time you get to them. Second tip: If doing only one ear, it will take a little *more* than half as long as two ears; three ears will not quite take three times as long as one ear, etc. One large ear may take 6 minutes or more.

To microwave husked corn: If corn is only partially husked, finish the job. Rinse ears thoroughly in cold water (it no longer came to you in its protective wrapper), shake off excess, and roll in a paper towel to dry, but don't be too fanatical about it. Roll each ear up in a fresh paper towel, tucking in ends of towel as you go up, and cook as for unhusked, noting that it will take slightly less time—perhaps 30 seconds to a minute less per ear. Unwrap and serve; keep remaining ears wrapped up.

Variations: Nothing could possibly be an improvement.

Yield: As a side dish, allow 1-2 ears per person; as a main luncheon dish, allow 1-4 ears, depending on size of both ears and appetite.

Nutritional data: A small ear weighs about half a pound with its husks and silk, or about a third of a pound without; a medium ear, about 11-12 ounces with husk, half a pound without; large ears can approach a pound fully clothed or 10-12 ounces naked.

PER MEDIUM EAR

Protein..4g
Carbohydrates............................ 28g
Fat...1.2g
Calories...120
Fat by Calories 9.4%

Serving suggestion: For lunch, I like to add a green vegetable, such as green beans, broccoli, or greens; in hot weather, a tossed salad is a pleasing contrast in color, texture and temperature.

What if you don't have a microwave at work? I'd almost be willing to buy a small one, I enjoy this lunch so much; unfortunately, cooked corn loses an awful lot in refrigeration and reheating, by any method, so just have it at home, on weekends and as a side dish, especially with something like shamburgers (pages 13, 14).

What if you don't have one at home either? Then boil it until *just* done (adding nothing to the water, of course), bake, wrapped in foil, in oven or over coals, and accept my sympathy.

Incidentally, the aroma of your corn cooking in the lunchroom at work (which, unlike couscous, is something familiar, to which your fellow workers *can* relate) is not the only thing that will drive them crazy. Once I was chowing down happily on three good-sized ears, plus my usual veggie on the side, when a co-worker came in and exclaimed, "How can you eat so much and stay so skinny?"

"Eat so much?" I answered. "This corn and these green beans total about 400 calories or so. You've got a burger, fries, and a cola—that's around 1,200 calories. What I want to know is, how can *you* eat so much and then ask me how I stay so skinny?"

She looked at the satisfaction I was obviously receiving, envying the sheer quantity of food as well as the smell, and looked back to her tasteless, mayo-slathered burger (and then, surreptitiously, at her waistline). "Yeah, I guess you're right," she mumbled. A few months later, she was bringing tomato sandwiches on whole wheat to work. (Why she couldn't bring her own corn, I don't know. The microwave was there for everyone to use.)

Roots (Your Vegetables—Not Your Ancestors)

Perhaps you don't share my passion for corn on the cob, or perhaps you don't have access to the good stuff, either temporarily, due to the season, or (horrors) anytime. Fear not. Other simple, quick-cooking starches will form an excellent base for lunch—again, accompany with your favorite green veggie or tossed salad.

On page 10, I stated that a microwaved potato does not match an oven-baked one for crispness and flakiness. True, but a fresh-cooked lunch is still better than a reheated one, and a micro-baked potato, if you have the facilities at work, is a hot, satisfying lunch. (If you're eating at home, bake the thing in the oven.)

On the other hand, winter squashes, sweet potatoes, and yams (the terms are not interchangeable, but they're confused by everyone, including the guy who sells them and, therefore, me) do not have that flakiness so sought in the spud. Their softer, creamier texture suffers not from the microwave. Eating a really good, sweet squash or sweet potato is almost like eating pie filling. Here's how to do them all:

For potatoes, sweet potatoes, and yams: Clean and pierce several times with a fork. (To take to work, clean at home and wrap. Pierce just before cooking.) Microwave on full power for about 4 minutes for the smallest potatoes (about 4 ounces), about 6 minutes for medium (up to 1/2 pound), and 8 minutes for large (12 ounce). If doing larger quantities, figure about 8-10 minutes per pound. Turn and rotate halfway through. Check for doneness by piercing deeply with a fork or knife; if still not tender, return to oven. See seasoning suggestions for potatoes on page 15; the others need nothing else, although those who used to like candied sweet potatoes may want to add a dash of cinnamon. Or add a lot of cinnamon, put it between two pieces of whole-wheat bread and call it a pie.

For squash: My favorite is buttercup (not butternut) squash, a deep green variety which, when fresh, is extremely sweet. Watch out for mottling, mold, or rot, indicating old ones which may be bitter. Since they are much larger than potatoes, they should be split in half, or they will take too long to cook. You may do this at home, scooping out the seeds and wrapping the halves in plastic wrap, if there is a refrigerator at work; otherwise bring a knife and prepare them at work. Place them on a microwavable plastic dish to catch juices and wrap tightly, face up. Cook on full power, rotating halfway through; a 3-4 pound squash will require about 8 minutes for one half or about 15 minutes for both halves. Sitting time is important to assure thorough cooking; allow squash to sit, still tightly wrapped, for 5 minutes or so, during which time you can cook your side vegetable. Potatoes and yams do not absolutely require this sitting time, but are often improved by it, so you can use the time thusly with them, also. (Don't worry, all of these will stay plenty hot.) Note: It doesn't seem to be widely known, but if

5—L.C.

your squash is really fresh and sweet, you can eat the skin also, for a change of taste and texture with a bite of pulp.

If you have a hot plate but no microwave at work, you need not be "rootless" (ouch!). Boil and mash potatoes, as per page 15, or bake, peel, and mash yams or squash at home and reheat over low heat in a tightly-covered saucepan at work. Unmashed, boiled potatoes ("parsley potatoes") can also be reheated this way, but it takes more time and water since they are denser and you can't stir them around as well.

By the way, if you're having sweet potatoes, yams, or squash at home, you can get a nice, crisp crust (skin) on the sweet potatoes or yams by baking them in the oven instead of microwaving; squash doesn't seem to be affected (and most people don't eat the skin) so there's no reason to waste the energy and heat up the kitchen if you have the alternative.

Broiled Leftover Potatoes

This isn't really something you can do at work, since it requires a broiler (unless you have a toaster oven—what do you do, work in a restaurant or something?), but it's a good item to include here because it makes a great lunch or side dish and is also a sterling way to use any leftover or microwaved potatoes.

Slice cold, cooked potatoes about an eighth inch thick. Place in single layer on nonstick baking sheet coated with nonstick vegetable spray. Broil on top rack until brown, turn, and brown second side, about 5 minutes each side. Serve immediately. Keep extras in warm oven.

These come out so nice and crunchy, they're almost as good as French fries (page 14), though they lack the souffled effect. They don't seem to ask for any salt, either, so try them as a first-run alternative to the air-fries, by prebaking and cooling raw potatoes, if you're on a low-sodium diet.

"Roots" Yield and Nutritional Data

Potatoes: Figure 1/2-1 pound per person as a luncheon or side dish, depending, of course, on whether anything else is served.

See page 15 for nutritional data on potatoes, all cooking methods.

Sweet potatoes and yams: Allow as for potatoes, but strict calorie-counters should note that their higher sugar content makes them about 20-25 percent more caloric than potatoes.

Squash: The dieter's choice. The higher water content and less-dense flesh makes them about half as caloric as potatoes and a little over a third as caloric as the other two, yet exceedingly filling and satisfying. Allow 1-2 pounds per person; if you've made a large squash and have some left over, wrap tightly and refrigerate, and reheat in microwave, foil-wrapped in oven, or mashed in a pot as suggested on the previous page.

SWEET POTATOES, PER POUND

Protein	6g
Carbohydrates	97g
Fat	1.5g
Calories	419
Fat by Calories	3.2%

YAMS, PER POUND

Protein	8g
Carbohydrates	91g
Fat	0.8g
Calories	394
Fat by Calories	1.8%

SQUASH, PER POUND

Protein	5g
Carbohydrates	40g
Fat	1g
Calories	161
Fat by Calories	5.6%

Note: These tables were prepared on the assumption that you will not eat the skin. Doing so would increase values slightly per pound.

Nuts and Berries (Wheat and Rye Berries, That Is)

Whenever Yogi Bear was prohibited from filching picnic (picanic?) baskets full of rich, fatty food, such as fried chicken, he turned glumly back to his natural bear's diet with some such comment as "Yecch! Nuts and berries!" The phrase has come to be a metaphor for a natural, healthful, but sparse diet, at least until the late Nathan Pritikin pointed out that nuts were too fatty, and all that was left was berries.

He was being facetious, and by now you, too, know that a healthful diet can be incredibly varied and tasty. But simple fare has its appeal, too, especially for portable, easily-reheatable lunch items and *especially* if dinner is going to be elaborate or spicy. (There's no reason you couldn't have these as a dinner staple, and I have done so often, but I've gotten spoiled with all my fancy concoctions.)

What are we talking about, anyway? We laugh at the city child who thought that milk came from a carton, not from a cow, but how many of us ever stop to think about, or even know, where wheat comes from, other than a bag of flour? In chapter 8, we introduced bulgur, a less-refined form of wheat than flour; now let's go all the way back to the beginning.

You've seen pictures or movies of stalks of wheat waving in fields in Kansas (or on a Wheaties box or in Canada but usually not in the Soviet Union). Separate out the chaff, as the saying goes, and you are left with wheat berries, or seeds, little nuggets of either reddish-brown or off-white. These can be blanched, dried, and cracked into bulgur, as we have seen, or, more typically, milled into flour, or, even more typically, milled, degermed, debranned, and chemically bleached into the yummy white flour in your croissants. We, however, are going to use the berries as Nature grew them.

Rye berries are about the same size as wheat berries, which is to say, not quite the size of short-grain brown rice, but they are tan or almond-colored. Both are available at any health-food store worthy of the name, where you may also find berries of triticale, a cross between wheat and rye. Just as in their respective breads, you will find rye berries to be a little stronger and nuttier in flavor than wheat, which is a little sweeter. (There's also certainly no reason why you can't mix the two, in any proportion you desire, for any use which either of them would fulfill.)

Well, we've got these berries; now what do we do with them? That's easy. Simmer, covered, in three cups water to each cup of berries, for an hour, stirring once or twice. Drain in a colander (all the water will not be absorbed) and serve, with veggies or salad on the side. I prefer not to add any spices—there is nothing which is closer to the elemental essence of grain flavor, and I like to savor it. I will momentarily, however, give a recipe for mixing in fresh vegetables.

You can also microwave the berries, using the same cooking technique as for brown rice (page 27), but with the water increased as above. You could also make a very pretty "freckled" rice by using one cup of each to 5 cups of water, but you'll probably have to pour off a bit of water at the end.

Wheat or rye berries may also be served where any other grain is called for, such as rice, millet, or bulgur, but be advised that they are much less absorbent than these other grains and so will not sop up juices the way that, say, millet does under stuffed grape leaves (page 53).

This same lack of absorbency means that they keep, transport, and reheat very well. Refrigerate cooked berries in a bowl covered with plastic wrap; they reheat equally well in the microwave with a tablespoon or so of water added per cooked cup, or in a covered saucepan with a bit more water, simmered over moderate heat. They are not very prone to spoilage; if you brought them to work well-chilled, in an airtight container, you probably would need no refrigerator, cooler, or even thermal bag, as long as they were kept in a cool place and for not more than a few hours.

Yield: One cup of raw berries equals about three cups cooked; allow 1/3-1/2 cup of raw berries per person as a lunch dish, or as much as one cup per person if used as the main grain of dinner.

PER RAW CUP

Protein.. 21g
Carbohydrates............................. 122g
Fat.. 3.1g
Calories 561
Fat by Calories........................... 4.9%

Note: Values are for hard red winter wheat; rye is almost identical. Soft red winter wheat and white wheat (berries, not flour!) have a bit less protein and a bit more fat and carbs, while hard red spring wheat has more protein and fat and fewer carbs. None of the differences are significant, and if you buy red berries, you're probably not going to know which variety you're getting anyway. It may interest you to know, however, that durum wheat, which is often used in conventional, white-flour spaghetti, has over 37 percent more fat than hard red winter wheat! The refining process, which removes the wheat germ and thereby a good bit of the fat, is what makes white spaghetti a very low-fat, if overly refined, product.

Wheat Berries With Fresh Vegetables

Here's a way to flavor your berries up a bit, either for lunch or when you're in the mood for a simple, easy-to-fix dinner. (It could all be done in one dish, if you microwave the berries and then use the same bowl or casserole for the combination; or, slightly less desirable, the same saucepan in which berries were cooked on stove.) This is also a great brown-bag item, although since there are cut-up fresh veggies involved, you'll need either a refrigerator at work or an insulated brown bag.

1 c. raw berries (wheat, rye, or any combination thereof), cooked as per page 67.
1 lb. sliced raw zucchini and/or yellow squash (cut slices in half if large in diameter)

Place veggies on top of cooked, drained berries in microwave bowl (preferable) or saucepan. Cook on full power 5-8 minutes, stirring once (or simmer, covered, with a little water added, over moderate heat on stove), until veggies are tender. Serve immediately. Serves 2-3 at lunch; 1-2 at dinner.

Variations: Zucchini and yellow squash are far and away my favorites for this, as they produce copious juices in which the berries steam, but you could also use broccoli, asparagus, greens (mustard, turnip, or collard), or any other vegetable with a good, strong flavor to lend to the berries.

No Place to Heat Your Lunch? Hey, What a Mean Boss You Have!

This is the more typical brown-bagging situation, especially for those who work outside of an office type location. Again, it subdivides into two categories: hot lunch or cold? No, the barrenness of your workplace shall not leave you bereft of a hot lunch! (I spent my office-rat years in Florida, but the place was so over-airconditioned that I always wanted a hot lunch.) On the other hand, a cold lunch is just the thing for days at the beach, warm-weather picnics or hikes, or at outdoor job sites in the summer. (When I did construction work during college summers in the same state, hot lunches were definitely *not* appealing.) Or you may be lucky enough to work in an office whose air-conditioning does not require you to wear a sweater.

Let's look at hot lunches first. You may be surprised to find that you have many of the same choices as those blessed with cooking facilities at work. The key here is the modern, vacuum-insulated, wide-mouth container. With it you have the same flexibility simply to use a previous night's leftovers for lunch. Here's how:

While your breakfast is cooking or while you're dressing or whatever, fill the vacuum bottle with hot tap water (boiling water from the kettle if you really want to get fancy), and allow to sit, lightly covered. Meanwhile, heat food in microwave or on stove as applicable. Heat it thoroughly—to bubbling, if possible—without scorching. When through with breakfast, empty water from vacuum bottle and immediately add still-bubbling food; insert stopper tightly. You may find at lunchtime that you can still burn your mouth.

Some tips: The less air space there is in the bottle, the hotter the food will stay. Vacuum bottles come in several sizes; it wouldn't be a bad investment to purchase at least two different capacities so you can match the quantity of food more closely to the bottle. (Also, you'll have more carrying capacity for multi-person picnics, etc. They won't go to waste.)

You must also choose your food a little more carefully than one who has the luxury of later reheating. The foods which stay the hottest are those which have considerable liquid to hold heat and to exclude air spaces between food particles. Obviously, shamburgers aren't going to work, whereas something such as spaghetti with mushroom sauce is ideal—it can be heated to boiling, if you stir frequently, and the thick tomato purée stays hot for hours. Others which work well are ratatouille and curried vegetables (be sure you save all the broth from each, and go ahead and reheat veggies and rice together), sloppy joes (the bread will be at room temperature, but the hot filling will take care of that), and chili.

Foods lacking so much liquid or sauce but which can be packed densely will also work fairly well, such as couscous, chow mein, rice pilaf (and variations), fried rice, and taco casserole (bring the garnish in a separate cold bag). A trick which helps here is to add some water during reheating, thinning the food a bit but immeasurably assisting heat retention. If you have enough broth or don't mind the milder flavor caused by adding water you could use this technique on grape leaves. I haven't yet figured out a way, though, to pack baked stuffed eggplant into a thermal bottle. (I suppose you could empty out and reheat the stuffing, with water, and pack it in the bottle, and put the eggplant shells in the sun when you get to work, but now we're getting a little ridiculous.) Best bet: cut it into bite-sized pieces, heat and pack into bottle.

One last tip: When you are ready to eat, stir the food around a bit, especially if there was much air space at the top. The top layer of food may be a bit cool, while that underneath, which did not come in contact with the air, will be much hotter.

Back to Our "Roots"

You can play "hot potato" at work or on picnics, etc., even without your portable solar cooker. The result doesn't quite match a fresh-baked spud, but it's an enormously satisfying, energy-boosting hot (well, warm) lunch, and its compactness and light weight make it ideal carry-along food for hikers and campers. (Besides, at the beach everything gets so covered with sand that everything tastes the same anyway—namely, gritty.)

The technique is the same for potatoes, yams, or squash. As soon as you get up in the morning (or whenever), flick the oven on, clean the food, and pierce with a fork a few times. Throw them in the oven and go about your business—don't worry about letting it

get to preheated temperature. If you're like me, by the time you've dressed, eaten, and gotten everything packed (especially for the beach), an hour will have gone by, and the food will be ready. (Very large squashes may take longer, so try to buy several of the smaller ones—under 2 pounds, if possible—instead.) Remove it from the oven (carefully) and immediately wrap in several layers of aluminum foil. Place in paper bag (or insulated hot thermal bag if you have one), wrap down tightly, and put in the trunk of your car, unless it's cold enough that you'll be running the heater. At work, keep in a warm place, such as near the coffeepot and away from air-conditioning vents. (Also keep it away from yourself, or the smell will drive you nuts and make you hungry by 10:30 a.m. Let your co-workers suffer instead.) On hikes, etc., just stuff them in your backpack with everything else; the pack and its contents provide further insulation. At the beach or on outdoor jobsites leave in the car trunk, on the dashboard or rear windshield deck in the sun (your car will smell like potatoes for a while afterward, which may make you hungry while driving), or, best of all, just out in the sun on your beach blanket or near your work area. (If you're working outdoors in cold weather, leave in car as above; or, if that's not practical, because, say, you'll be eating lunch on the girders of a sixty-story skyscraper, just throw it in your basic, typical lunch pail and carry it with you.)

Ease of consumption is another major advantage of this repast. In an office, you can get fancy, with a knife and fork if you wish, but outdoors, just eat it like a banana, peeling back the foil a little at a time and munching from the end. Sprinkle on your favorite seasoning, if desired, as you go down. You will find the flavor a bit different from a fresh-baked potato, with a creamy, instead of flaky, texture, and of course the skin won't be crisp, but it's surprisingly good. Try it!

Note: You noticed this is *not* the time to cut your squash in half before baking it, so be sure to bring a sharp knife to cut it, and a fork or spoon to remove the seeds and eat it—the banana trick is not going to work here.

What if you dress and eat a lot quicker than that or eat breakfast on the train or in the car pool or (shame on you!) don't eat breakfast? In other words, what if you haven't got an hour in the morning? A microwave can still render this method feasible. Turn on the oven, throw the food in the microwave for half to two-thirds of the time needed for full cooking (see guidelines on page 65) while you dress or whatever, then put the food in the (now thoroughly preheated) oven. It will take only a third to a half of the normal baking time, while still developing a nice flavor in the skin and flesh. (If you're *really* rushed—if you're the type who wakes up, throws on clothes, and runs out the door—you can do all of the cooking in the microwave, but you'll get a steamed, rather than baked, effect, which is compounded by the sitting time.) You can save a minute or two of additional time by having the food cleaned, but not pierced, the night before.

If you have no microwave, but still need a timesaving method, bake the food the night before (fully), cool and refrigerate, then reheat in the oven, wrapped in foil, for 15-20 minutes or so the next morning. Now you don't even have to wrap them when they come out!

If none of these ideas fits your schedule, see the suggestions under cold lunches.

IMPORTANT CAUTION: This technique is for use only for periods not to exceed 4 hours, e.g. heated in the morning, eaten at lunch (food should still be warm). According to researchers at the University of California (Berkeley), leaving cooked potatoes at room temperature, foil-wrapped, for 12-24 hours was responsible for a case of potentially fatal botulism poisoning. The potatoes in question had been left out overnight (cooked and wrapped), then used the next day to make cold potato salad. This is a no-no.

Barley-Vegetable Soup

Soup is another natural and favorite choice for a hot lunch. Obviously, it could have been included in the section on lunches to reheat at work, but its perfect suitability for the vacuum-bottle method makes it desirable to add to our list here, where the selection is somewhat more limited. (If you do have reheating facilities at work, it's just a question of whether you'd rather take the time to heat it at home or at work.)

Don't forget leftover minestrone (page 36), another ideal vacuum-bottle filler. That soup was included in the Dinners section of the book because its content of beans and pasta makes it substantial enough to serve as a main course. This soup is much lighter and therefore makes an ideal lunch. Of course, you may also serve it as a first course before most of the dinners listed; besides being a tasty appetizer, starting with soup is a well-known calorie-reducing technique available to dieters who find, somehow, that they're not losing weight fast enough just by eating these dinners by themselves.

Soup is also convenient in that it can be made in bulk on an evening or weekend and refrigerated or even frozen for a week's worth of lunches. To freeze, pour into airtight plastic containers, using several smaller ones for convenient thawing quantities, and leaving a little air space at the top. Plan ahead for thawing—it takes a day or more in the refrigerator or several hours in a bath of lukewarm water. You may speed this up considerably if you are willing to give it some attention, by plopping the frozen block in a saucepan or suitable covered microwave dish. Simmer, covered, over low heat, or microwave on 1/4-1/3 power ("Low" or "Defrost"), in either case stirring frequently, to break thawed portions off and prevent burning the thawed soup. Under either method, you may increase the heat somewhat as the soup gets closer to being thawed and ice portion decreases.

There is only one basic vegetable-soup recipe here for the same reason that there is only one basic chow mein recipe. The choice of ingredients is really yours, and virtually any combination of cut-up vegetables will work. The recipe gives one combination which I like and provides guidelines as to quantity; you may substitute freely from there. Cookbook authors who give a number of vegetable soup recipes, each differing by only a few ingredients, are, in my opinion, just padding their work. I consider your time to be much more valuable than that.

1 large onion, chopped
3 large ribs celery, chopped
2 large carrots, chopped

1 16-oz. can tomatoes, with juice,
 chopped
1 medium (1/2 lb.) potato, peeled and
 diced
1/2 lb. fresh mushrooms, cleaned and
 chopped
1/2 c. barley
1 tbsp. dill weed
1 tbsp. sage
2 tbsp. parsley flakes
1 tbsp. thyme
1 tsp. rosemary
1 tsp. white pepper
1 tsp. to 1 tbsp. or more black pepper,
 to taste
3 bay leaves
6 c.water

Combine all ingredients in large pot (5-quart size or larger). Bring to a boil, cover, reduce heat, and simmer, stirring occasionally, for one to several hours, making sure all ingredients are tender. Check seasoning occasionally and add if necessary.

Serving suggestion: For a more substantial lunch, serve with cornbread (page 78), perhaps adding fresh fruit or a tossed salad. For a very filling, ultra-low calorie diet lunch, serve with tossed salad.

Yield: As an appetizer, serves 4-8; at lunch, serves 4-6 or more, depending on accompaniments.

PER 1/6 RECIPE

Protein 4g
Carbohydrates 26g
Fat...0.5g
Calories...122
Fat by Calories............................3.7%

Variation: In addition to vegetable variations as mentioned in the discussion, a thicker, more substantial soup may be made by adding 1/4-1/2 cup of raw brown rice at the start. This will add 25-50 calories per serving.

Cold Lunches

You may desire a cold lunch, but as we've seen, you certainly needn't be forced into one by circumstances. An ice chest is nice, but bulky to lug around; the insulated bags mentioned earlier can do almost as good a job,

for reasonable periods of time.

One of my favorite uses of cold lunches is for long car trips. While driving in cold weather might call for warm foil-wrapped potatoes (which can be eaten while you drive if you're really careful, or have someone feed you), a long drive in warm weather seems to invite a chance to get out and stretch and have a refreshing cold lunch at a wayside table. (I drive through the town of Wayside Table almost as frequently as I pass the town of Litter Barrel.) Whatever the circumstances, here are a few ideas.

Roots, Part III

What, potatoes *again?* Remember on page ?? I said that if none of the methods for taking warm potatoes to lunch suited you, then you should investigate the cold lunch ideas? Well, potatoes and sweet potatoes can simply be eaten cold. (Squash isn't quite as appetizing.) Cook your potatoes the night before, or use leftovers from dinner and refrigerate overnight. Wrap them in foil and carry in cooler, insulated bag or a plain paper bag. They're fine whether they stay cold or get closer to room temperature. (If you decide you don't like them cold, just throw them in a paper bag, and they should be close to room temperature by lunchtime. Starches don't spoil so quickly—it's fats, such as meat and butter, which turn rancid.) Try it; it really works. And I promise that's the very last time I'm going to mention potatoes in the entire book.

Rabbit Food

I wish people wouldn't use the term negatively. Rabbits rarely get heart disease, and as for their procreative abilities—well, never mind. And if the term refers to boring eating, I guarantee my recipes, given later, will fix that!

Salads serve double duty—they are a traditional side dish at dinner and have been recommended as such many times in this volume, but they are also a favorite at lunch. Dieters love them because in terms of crunch, fillingness (to coin a word), and taste, not to mention nutrition, they are about as "cheap" in calorie "cost" as you are ever going to get. The rest of us add bread, crackers (suggestions later), or soup for a nourishing, satisfying lunch. In a little bit, I'll have a complete section on salad and cole slaw, plus recipes for breads and other accompaniment ideas, which you may combine as you wish. But first, here's a fancy, meal-in-itself salad which is easy to make the night before and take along virtually anywhere.

Cold Rice Salad

This is one of my favorites for picnics or car trips.

1 c. raw brown rice, or 3 c. leftovers
2 medium carrots, peeled and sliced
    into discs
1/2 of a 10-oz. package of frozen peas
1/2 of a 10-oz. package of frozen
    asparagus cuts and tips
1/2 of a 10-oz. package of frozen broc-
    coli
1/2 of a 14-oz. can of artichoke hearts
    (not oil-packed or marinated),
    drained, rinsed, and drained
    again (to reduce salt content
    from packing fluid)
1/2-1 medium red onion, to taste,
    minced
4-6 medium radishes, sliced
1 large or 2 medium tomatoes, cut
    into small wedges
1/4-1/2 c. of 50/50 mix of vinegar and
    lemon juice
Basil
Oregano

Start rice cooking, if applicable; thaw vegetables at room temperature or in microwave, but do not allow to cook. Cut broccoli, artichokes, and asparagus into bite-sized pieces, if necessary. If using fresh-cooked rice, pour vinegar over it as soon as it is done; then add vegetables and seasonings. (It seems to absorb a more pungent aroma this way.) Otherwise, simply combine all ingredients, adding spices to taste. The flavor is better if allowed to sit for a while rather than being made just before lunch, which—happy coincidence—is perfect for our brown-bag purposes. The best and most convenient method is to

make it the night before and refrigerate—it's ready to pack along the next morning or to eat at home.

Yield: At lunch, serves 2-4 very well.

PER 1/4 RECIPE

Protein.................................... 10g
Carbohydrates........................... 54g
Fat...1.4g
Calories..................................260
Fat by Calories 5%

Variations: Add or substitute one or more of the following: sliced cucumber, julienned red and/or green bell pepper, fresh raw cauliflower florets.

Salads, Breads, and Vegetables

The remainder of this chapter will be devoted to recipes which really can't be pinned down to lunch or dinner, or to a meal at all—they can serve as, or accompany, lunch or dinner, or be used as between-meal or midnight snacks. Some have been referred to earlier in the text; others are making their first appearance. Enjoy them all, wherever and whenever you like.

Cole Slaw

The perennial picnic favorite (minus the oil or mayo, of course), this also makes a fitting side to shamburgers or sloppy joes. It's another recipe which benefits from sitting time, so make it the night before, chill well, and pack along; or make earlier in the day to serve at lunch or dinner.

1 small head cabbage, or 1/2 large
    head (about 1 1/2 lbs.), cored
2 large or 3 medium carrots, peeled
Vinegar
Prepared mustard
Garlic powder

Shred cabbage into very large mixing bowl, probably the same one you used for stuffed cabbage (page 54). Peel off ribbons of carrot with a vegetable peeler; then cut these into 1-2 inch lengths. When you can't peel any more off the carrot, slice the remainder into bite-sized pieces. Add carrot to bowl.

Add vinegar, mustard, and spices. There is really no way to specify quantity of each, as individual taste will vary widely, but you might start with 1/4 cup vinegar, 1 tablespoon mustard, and a few shakes/grindings of the spices. Mix thoroughly. Taste. This will no doubt be too mild. (I like about three times this much, but it's better to start too light, especially until you've made it a few times.) Add a little more of each, mix, and retaste. Eventually you'll taste that you want to add only one or two ingredients instead of all four. Allow for the fact that it will get a little more pungent as it sits. Before serving, mix well and, if possible, recheck seasoning. (But don't bother lugging them along on your picnic, or whatever, especially after you have a little experience and can judge what the "aged" product will taste like.) Try to remember, or write down, the proportions you liked, so it will be a little quicker next time; but since your next head of cabbage may be larger or smaller, this is always a taste-as-you-go affair anyway. (Let's face it, we great chefs always work like that—I rarely measure spices in anything, after initially developing a recipe.)

Yield: As a side dish, serves 4-6 or more. Leftovers may be refrigerated, in airtight plastic containers or tightly covered with plastic wrap, for several days; makes a great addition to a brown-bag lunch. Note: Stir well before apportioning leftovers, because vinegar will settle to bottom of bowl during storage.

PER 1/4 RECIPE

Protein 3g
Carbohydrates 12g
Fat...0.8g
Calories.. 58
Fat by Calories...........................11.7%

(If you wonder how this managed to be the first recipe in the book to crawl into double digits in the percent-calories-from-fat category, the answer is that mustard seed, like most seeds and nuts, is rather high in fat, proportionately; I use mustard where appropriate because the quantity required is so small. That 11.7 percent figure still meets every medical/diet recommendation I've ever seen and makes the American Heart Association's 30 percent-fat guideline seem

positively gluttonous by comparison. The mustard swings the figures so much because cabbage is so low in calories; the same amount of mustard on a couple of shamburgers or in chow mein would be diluted by the greater amount of carbohydrates in these foods and therefore affect the final data much less.)

Tossed Salad

We had a dinner guest once (a carnivore) who upon being served one of our tossed salads with dinner remarked, "Wow, your salads are different from ours. They've got—so many *ingredients!*"

We still haven't figured out why they can't put lots of ingredients in their salads at home (they enjoyed ours immensely), any more than I can figure out why my envious co-workers couldn't bring their own corn to work and cook it in the communal microwave. In any event, it's got to be the standard iceberg-lettuce-and-plastic-tomato pile, served in restaurants and imitated at home (perhaps with a slice of cucumber or onion), which gives salads the bad name mentioned earlier and makes dieters feel deprived.

So what do you put in your tossed salad? Start with a little iceberg lettuce if you must (it's the lowest in nutrition and flavor of the lettuces; I skip it completely), but add leaf lettuce (red or green), romaine, or bibb; endive and escarole tend to be bitter, but a few shreds can go in also. Next add sliced cucumber (unfortunately, you should peel it if the skin is waxed, which it usually is) and yellow squash. Now some sliced carrot and, optional (but awfully good), bell peppers. Don't limit yourself to green and/or red peppers; many supermarkets are now carrying additional varieties such as yellow or gold and purple bell peppers. The former taste sweet, closer to red peppers; the latter are more similar to green. (Incidentally, shop around carefully for these relatively recent introductions, where competition may not be widespread yet; I've seen yellow bell peppers offered at $5.99/pound in one supermarket, while a produce store in the same vicinity had them for 39¢/pound.)

For a change from regular onions, try the sweeter red variety, or, one of my favorites, use sliced green onions instead. (Discard the leafy green tops.) Sliced radishes will now add the pungency needed to offset the sweetness of the carrots, peppers and onions.

You're hardly done yet. Break up or cut some fresh cauliflower florets into bite-sized pieces and add to your rapidly bulging bowl; then chop up that cored, very ripe beefsteak tomato for which you hunted all over town to find a supplier. (You can buy them unripe and let them sit on the counter in a paper bag, so that you have a freshly ripe one every day or so. Refrigerate ripe ones or leftover sections in a paper bag in the vegetable drawer, wrapping cut pieces tightly in plastic wrap or a plastic bag.)

A "Hearty" Ingredient

Now open a can of hearts of palm (Floridians know it as swamp cabbage, but this sounds much fancier) and of artichoke hearts. The latter are most often sold in jars as "marinated," which means in oil. Look carefully, in the gourmet section, and you should find cans of both packed only in water, salt, and citric acid, which seems safe enough, since it's an ingredient in oranges. Drain only the quantity of each needed (one artichoke and half a palm heart per salad should do), rinse under cold running water, and drain again. I'm extremely salt-sensitive, and I can hardly discern any salt taste in the rinsed product, so that should accommodate all but the very-sodium-restricted. (The latter please check with your doctor first, so I don't get into trouble.) Slice the palm hearts into discs and cut each artichoke heart into quarters, sixths, or eighths, according to size, and scatter over tomatoes. Place remaining ones in (separate) airtight plastic containers, pour their packing juice over them, and refrigerate until needed.

For a final garnish and to add real zip to the entire package, consider pepperoncini (Greek salad peppers), mild or hot cherry peppers (or both, as I do), or, for the really adventurous, hot banana or yellow chili peppers. All of these, however, call for even more intense label perusal. Not only oil, but sweeteners such as corn syrup may be used in packing these, not to mention preservatives and even food coloring. At one time, I was using pepperoncini packed in water, vinegar, salt, and sodium bisulfite. A good deal of controversy had arisen over sulfites, however, so I thought it would be an improvement when I found a brand whose ingredient table listed water, vinegar, salt, and polysorbate 80. I thought so, that is, until I later looked at the rest of the label and found, completely separate from the list of ingredients, "Sodium bisulfite added to preserve color." I had not traded one chemical for another; I had added one needlessly! Fortunately, there is a happy ending—shortly thereafter, I saw a bottle of mild cherry peppers which contained (I examined the label with a microscope) only water, vinegar, and salt.

Rinse the peppers thoroughly, and not only drain, but pat dry with a paper towel, so you won't have a watery salad. The same comments on sodium restriction apply as a couple of paragraphs ago; these may be packed in a little saltier water, or perhaps absorb more, because I can sometimes detect a trace of saltiness, although the pepper and vinegar flavors by far predominate.

If you don't care for peppers, or the doctor says not to, increase the radishes and seasonings. Either way, you'll have a salad which is a veritable cornucopia of colors, tastes, textures, and nutrition—anything but boring. You, too, can be the envy of the lettuce-and-tomato crowd.

How do you eat the thing? I don't toss mine; I like the effect of the different-colored layers, and, besides, the bowl's too full. So I start at the top and tunnel through with my fork. You can't possibly get some of everything in every bite, which makes each bite different from the previous—think of the suspense!

Don't feel constrained, of course, to use exactly these ingredients. Leave out any you don't like (hey, how am I going to know, anyway?) and add any others which sound appealing, such as, for example, fresh raw broccoli or zucchini. Yield is a moot point also—lay out the number of bowls you need and keep going until you fill them. (Beware the temptation to put in too much lettuce at first, later discovering that there's no room for the last few ingredients.) But serve *big* salads—mine average over 3 cups each. They're generally recommended in the dinner menus for their contrast to the main dish in terms of color, temperature, and especially textures—i.e. crunchiness—and the dieters will appreciate it too.

Speaking of dieters, nutritional data would also be hard to compute with such uncertain amounts of so many ingredients. Sweet, solid vegetables such as carrots and onions are relatively higher in calories (with "high" being taken in a low-calorie context), while lettuce is mostly air in your bowl. No matter what you mix in, 50 calories per cup, virtually all from carbohydrates, is probably a generous allowance, unless you really mash things down. In any event, I've never known anyone to get fat even from eating solid carrots and onions all day, and most diet plans allow (or demand) unlimited quantities of fresh vegetables and salads.

But, of course, we haven't dressed it yet.

What the Well-dressed Salad Will Wear

Many years ago, before we all knew everything about diet and health, as we don't now, an unnamed member of my family read that eating more salad before or with dinner would help lose weight. So the nightly salad, and the bowl in which it was contained, got larger and larger, growing like Topsy, until both reached gargantuan proportions. (Unfortunately, the portions of meat and potatoes never seemed to get any smaller, which I think was really the idea.) And on top of this mountain of greenery would go a proportionately large glop of commercial salad dressing, at 120 calories per ounce, most of them from fat (oil), much of the rest from sugar. Poor family member could never figure out why no weight was lost!

Salads are like pasta—they're not fattening, it's what you put on them that does the damage, a lot more damage than many people realize. Nowadays, we have commercial "reduced calorie" dressings and recipes for dieters to make their own at home. The former, while down to "only" 50 calories per ounce, still get most of their calories from fat and sugar (or other sweeteners), while the latter suffer gastronomically from their attempt to mimic the former in texture, appearance, and, sometimes, sweetness. A poor imitation of something is worse than nothing at all—as we saw, for example, in the hamburger recipes touted in other "vegetarian" cookbooks which use soybeans, nuts, cheese, oil, or other fatty ingredients to produce an appropriately greasy veggie-burger.

No, what must be done, just as with the vegetarian dinners, is to roll your own, starting from scratch, using the bountiful ingredients at hand to create your own taste delights, not an imitation of the junk sold in stores or served at restaurants. But it helps to have some kind of starting point, so let's take a look at the ingredients of a typical "low-cal" Italian dressing. It should be an eyeopener, and it may give us some ideas.

First on the list is water. I hope you're happy paying a dollar a bottle for something whose main ingredient is water. What's the point of carefully drying your greens if you're going to pour water on them anyway? We won't need *that* in our dressing.

Next is soybean oil, which provides over 70 percent of the calories. It doesn't look like much—just 2 grams of fat per serving—but look back at the dinner recipes in this book. Most of them average around 2 grams of fat per serving for the entire dinner! If you add one "serving," which is one tablespoon of this dressing, you've just *doubled* the fat content of your meal! And have you ever known anyone to use only one tablespoon of dressing on any decent-sized salad? We'll certainly skip the oil.

Now comes vinegar—the first shiningly virtuous ingredient. Vinegar is virtually calorieless—about 3 1/2 calories per ounce—and has lots of flavor. Let's keep it.

Right below vinegar we find high fructose corn syrup—translation: sugar (of one type or another). If you were going to munch a slice of cucumber, a carrot, or a tomato, perhaps for a snack, you probably would not sprinkle sugar on it first, so why put it on a combination of these items?

Next comes dehydrated sour cream. Once you get past the question of why they dehydrate some ingredients and then add water to the finished product (manufacturing convenience and cost, presumably), you're back to another high-fat ingredient, so out it goes.

Salt is next. No comment. Any saltiness you crave on your salad will be more than supplied by the canned and bottled salad ingredients, as we have seen.

Next on the list is—surprise!—sugar. By

using two different types of sweeteners (high fructose corn syrup and ordinary table sugar), each ranks lower in the list of ingredients than if they used an amount of one equal to the combined quantity of the two. (Corn syrup is also cheaper.)

The next three ingredients are two gums and a chemical for "consistency"—i.e. to mimic the creaminess of the really-high-fat, nondiet stuff. Then we have garlic juice—another flavoring, like vinegar, which is natural, tasty, and cheap in calories. But "lactic acid for tartness"? If they didn't put so much sugar in it you'd think that vinegar would be plenty tart!

Nonfat dry milk is, I suppose, for more creamy look and tastes, but this far down the list there can't be much of it; that's verified by the nutritional data on the label, which show zero protein. (Not that you need protein in your salad dressing, of course; it just shows there's not much milk.) but three useful items follow: dehydrated garlic, onion, and red bell peppers. I certainly like garlic and onion on my salads, but there are *real* bell peppers in mine, so I don't need the dehydrated kind.

Spices Unspecified

Now comes the unspecific item termed merely "spices." Some specific spices are listed later, so who knows what these could be, but it sounds good. Unfortunately, it's followed by "potassium sorbate, sodium benzoate, and calcium disodium EDTA to preserve freshness." Fortunately, since we're going to dress most of our salads freshly (and not use oils, sour cream, or other items which are vulnerable to rancidity), we won't need preservatives.

Last, and apparently least in the eyes of this manufacturer, are what are, to me, the most-important, not least-important, items: the general heading "Italian Seasonings." (I guess they call them that to justify calling it "Italian dressing.") Following, in parentheses, are the specifics: marjoram, thyme, rosemary, savory, sage, oregano, and basil. (See why I have no idea what were the "spices" listed earlier?) Even grouped together, rather than ranked individually (just the opposite of the trick they pulled with the sweeteners!), they're still last on the list, by quantity.

So what do we have? After we've gotten rid of the superfluous and undesirable items, we have vinegar, garlic, onion, and spices. Here's where the make-your-own advocates go wrong. Instead of being happy with that, they attempt to duplicate appearance or texture, as we have noted, by adding thickeners such as pectin or agar (a seaweed derivative), and usually water to combine with these, plus occasionally apple juice or another sweetener. It's still going to separate out after you shake it, since it doesn't have the chemical emulsifiers used for "consistency" in the commercial product, and the apple juice is going to taste funny on a salad. So what you end up with is a product which your mind thinks is supposed to look, feel (on your tongue), and taste like commercial dressing, and doesn't. You feel cheated.

What do you do? First, GET IT OUT OF YOUR HEAD THAT YOU HAVE TO HAVE SOMETHING IN A BOTTLE WHICH YOU SHAKE UP AND POUR ON SALADS. When we wanted to flavor our dinner recipes we didn't open a bottle and pour on flavorings, did we? Of course not. We used the real thing—herbs, spices, perhaps minced sweet or hot peppers—and added them directly to our food. And that's what we're going to do to our salad. Ready?

Step one: Sprinkle vinegar generously over your salad. How much is a matter of taste, but don't be stingy—I usually use about a tablespoon per cup of salad, or 1/4 cup for a 4-cup monster. And not just white vinegar, either—try the various herb vinegars such as tarragon, either by themselves or in any combination. Just varying which you use can make each salad different.

You may also use lemon juice instead of vinegar, or, for a special treat, how about a mustard vinaigrette: Mix 1/4-1/2 teaspoon Chinese mustard powder into vinegar before dressing salad. Zingy!

Step two: Shake garlic powder and onion powder until the entire top surface of the salad is dusted with each.

Step three: Add your spices (need I say, generously?). My favorites are oregano, basil, and marjoram, but follow the advice of our "wise" manufacturer and also experiment with rosemary, thyme, savory, sage, and perhaps even dill if you like its rather strong flavor. (I don't, on salads at least.) Again, cover the whole surface—you're going to tunnel through when you eat it, remember? (All right, toss it in a big bowl. See if I care.) I generally don't add my peppers to the salad until it has been seasoned, because the peppers really don't need any spices on them; I'd rather they fell on the tomatoes or whatever. The peppers (Greek, cherry, etc.) then make a crowning garnish.

The glorious result? You have a salad which, just like any other dish you cook, has been freshly flavored with just what it needs, at the time of its creation. And you have one in which the taste of the ingredients—the sweetness of the carrots and onions, the acidity of the tomatoes, the tang of any peppers, and perhaps a trace of bitterness in some of the greens—can come through and is enhanced by the dressing, instead of being lost beneath it, as is usually the case. And the calorie count? Perhaps five or six in the vinegar and microscopic quantities in the rest—so small, in total, that I hereby give you my official permission to disregard it completely. It would take a quart of this "dressing" to equal one ounce of the standard product or two ounces of the "low-cal." Ignore it and have salads as often as you wish, in any quantity, at any time of day.

BUT I NEED SOMETHING IN A BOTTLE TO TAKE TO WORK.

Fine. Take a bottle of vinegar. Carry along a little shaker of garlic powder, and one of onion powder, a little plastic bag with your herbs and you're all set. Or, even better, do what I do—make the salad the night before, dress it, and refrigerate it in an airtight plastic container.

WHAT! THE LETTUCE WON'T STAY CRISP!

Just as with the dressing itself, the problem is in your head. THINK OF IT AS MARINATED. Try this. Go to the grocery store. Look at the price of cucumbers, peppers, cauliflower, and carrots. Now go to the canned and bottled vegetable section. Look at the price of pickles and marinated vegetables. See what I mean? You're getting the same thing for free. And it will be a change of taste from your usual dinner salads.

HOW CLEVER! IT IS ALL IN HOW YOU LOOK AT IT. AND IT TASTES GREAT! BUT, YOU KNOW WHAT? WITH THE BOTTLED DRESSING I STILL HAD A VARIETY FROM WHICH TO CHOOSE, AND HERE I DON'T. I'D STILL LIKE A LITTLE MORE CHANGE OF TASTE ONCE IN A WHILE.

You mean, you had a variety of combinations of water, oil, vinegar, sugar, and salt to choose from? All right, if varying the spices you put on the salad isn't enough, try this, for a change not only of taste, but of texture as well.

Cooked Salad

This is especially appealing in cold weather, with a cooler dinner, or if you're not feeling well—most cooked vegetables are easier to digest than they are in their raw state. A microwave zips this out perfectly; you can use a steamer basket, but you'll lose the juice; a saucepan will do OK.

Assemble your entire salad, minus the tomatoes and garnishing peppers, if any. Dress it as above and cover tightly with plastic wrap. Microwave on half power for one minute (for 3-4 cups of salad), stir, add tomatoes and peppers, recover, and cook one more minute. Stir and serve immediately. Or simmer in tightly covered pot over very low heat (no water should be necessary) for a minute, stir, add tomatoes and peppers, and continue cooking for another minute, or until lettuce is wilted. Stir and serve.

Our Daily Bread

When I first began to reduce the amount of meat I ate, I started to eat a lot more bread—partly because it was filling, chewy, and familiar, and partly because I didn't yet know how else to replace the missing calories. At first I bought it at the supermarket. Not white bread, mind you, I knew better than that even then; nothing but rye and pumpernickel. Then, when I got into serious label-reading and saw that these still contained shortening or oils, sugar, and preservatives, I began to make it at home—often, several loaves a week. Eventually, the sheer time involved in baking every week became cumbersome. Fortunately, by that time I had acquired enough of a repertoire of dishes such as are in this book to provide plenty of other ways to get my filling grains.

I don't actually eat that much bread anymore, certainly not every day. And when I do, it's usually as a specific part of a meal, such as shamburger buns or as a snack. And for many meal usages, the health-food stores have come to the rescue of the busy, aware diner—buns and sub rolls, corn or whole-wheat tortillas, pizza crusts, even ordinary loaves of whole-grain or multi-grain bread, all made, as we have seen, without fats, oils, or preservatives, and with minimal or no sweeteners or salt. (When you buy these, READ THE LABEL. Reread page 13.) They've actually taken us back to the days when the phrase at the heading of this section was coined, when you actually could live on bread alone every day—whole grain bread, that is, not the air-fluff sold in most supermarkets.

Nevertheless, I do retain a couple of favorite bread recipes, which I'll pass along. I've never seen anything like them made commercially, and they're just right for snacks or with certain meals. Both are also ultra-quick and easy to make, with neither requiring a mixer, kneading, or rising. I'll also relay a few suggestions for other bread and snack items which you might not be aware of or have thought of.

Cornbread

This makes a great snack, either plain or toasted, and goes well, as has been suggested, with soup or salad for lunch, and with dishes such as chili at dinner. I've yet to see a commercial cornbread (or mix), in health-food stores or otherwise, that doesn't contain oil, sweeteners, and usually eggs; this one gets right down to the basics.

Note to the sodium-restricted: This and the following recipe, being for "quick" (non-yeast) breads, make use of baking powder. Check the figures in the tables and see if your doctor approves.

4 c. yellow cornmeal
2 c. whole-wheat flour
2 1/2 tbsp. baking powder
3 3/4 c. water

Preheat oven to 375°. Spray 2 nonstick 8- or 9-inch loaf pans or 8-inch square cake pans with nonstick vegetable spray. (The longer cooking time required by the deeper loaf pans gives the bread a crust that almost requires a buzz saw to cut through, but my, is that crust chewy and good!) Mix dry ingredients thoroughly in *large* mixing bowl. (see stuffed cabbage, page 54). Add water and stir thoroughly and quickly, but do not over-mix. Pour into pans and bake on middle rack for 30 minutes for square trays; 50 minutes for loaves. Check for doneness by inserting a toothpick into middle; if it does not come out dry, bake a few minutes longer and test again.

When done, let sit in pans on wire rack for 5 minutes, then invert pans onto racks, empty bread out, and let cool. Cut square bread into 16 squares; cut loaves (A serrated bread knife is best, if you don't have a buzz saw; cutting it upside-down often helps too. Believe me, the result is worth the effort.) into 16-20 slices, eating all the warm crumbs that fall out as part of your lunch.

Since the bread has no preservatives, any that is not to be eaten within a few days should be frozen. When slices have cooled completely, wrap loaf in plastic wrap and then in aluminum foil, and freeze.

To serve: If bread is already at room temperature, it is best if heated briefly, in microwave, toaster, or oven, or toasted until crisp and brown (it then smells like popcorn). You may wish to use a toaster oven or broiler for toasting bread, as it tends to crumble in your toaster. (All that fat in the store bread helps hold them together, as well as making the crust softer.)

If bread is frozen, pry apart desired number of slices with knife or fork. Thaw in microwave, wrapped in paper towel, on full power (not "Defrost" setting) for about one minute for one slice, a little less than a minute each for multiple slices; turn slices halfway through. If they are not nice and hot, return to microwave for a few seconds more, or toast as above.

Individual frozen slices may also be placed directly in toaster, broiler, etc., and toasted just until heated, or until crisp, as desired. You can also thaw and warm separated slices wrapped in foil in a 350° oven for 15 minutes or so, or allow it to thaw at room temperature, which takes about 1/2 hour, and heat as desired.

Nutritional data are based on 16 slices per loaf.

PER SLICE

Protein	3g
Carbohydrates	22g
Fat	0.4g
Calories	102
Fat by Calories	3.5%
Sodium	95mg

What to put on it, besides chili? Your tongue. For once, taste the corn flavor, not some sugary jelly or fatty spread.

Variation: For whole wheat bread, use all whole-wheat flour in place of cornmeal, keeping total quantity the same. Only square pans are recommended for this.

Oatmeal Bread

This is another one I don't find in the stores, unlike whole-wheat bread, for which there are many good, healthful versions. rather than being a meal accompaniment, this one seems to hit the spot all by itself, as a snack.

4 c. old-fashioned (not quick-cooking) rolled oats
3 c. water
1 tbsp. baking powder
2 2/3 c. whole-wheat flour

Soak oats in water in large mixing bowl for 30 minutes. (I use the same bowl as for the cornbread; in fact, I generally soak the oats while the cornbread bakes.) Preheat oven to 400°. Mix dry ingredients well in a smaller bowl. Spray two 8-inch nonstick loaf pans with nonstick vegetable spray. (Be careful handling and spraying the hot cornbread pans. And if no one peeks, they'll never know you didn't wash them in between.) Add dry mix to oats. Stir well until stiff and well-blended. Pour or spoon into pans; shake pans until dough is fairly level. Bake in center of oven 40-50 minutes or until toothpick inserted in center comes out clean. Cool, remove, cut, freeze, and serve as for cornbread.

PER SLICE

Protein	3g
Carbohydrates	13g
Fat	0.9g
Calories	68
Fat by Calories	11.7%
Sodium	38mg

Note: Oats have the highest fat content of the common grains. See discussion on page 73 of cole slaw, which has the same fat percentage as the oatmeal bread.

Other Bread and Snack Ideas

In addition to home-baked breads, here are a few more items which are handy to keep around the house for snacks or emergency munchies.

Corn tortillas can be turned into chips, for good snacking anytime, with "crunch" which often seems missing when you get away from fried foods. Keep a pack in the refrigerator or freezer.

Bagels, other than egg bagels, are generally fat-free, but check labels on store packages—I've seen a few, even in health-food stores, with soy oil in them. Whole-wheat bagels are increasingly common, even at your ordinary deli or bakery, and some brands sold in health-food stores have even eliminated the sugar and salt from the typical bagel recipe, consisting of nothing but whole-wheat flour, water, yeast, and flavorings (garlic, onion, whatever). these can be frozen and reheated quickly as needed, in microwave (about a minute each) or oven, and toasted under the broiler.

On an ethnically similar subject, the traditional matzo, which has always been a low-fat snack, consisting only of flour and water, has just been improved. I was delighted recently to find in my supermarket's kosher-foods section a package of whole-wheat matzos, made from stone-ground whole-wheat flour, wheat bran, and water. You couldn't ask for a better ingredient list than that; they go great with soups or salads, and it doesn't even matter what your religion is.

Getting away from bread, you can go less refined than corn tortillas and eat the corn itself. Buy an air-popper (or get one with stamps), the greatest invention for the health-conscious snacker since, I don't know, whole-wheat matzo? Popcorn, long a taboo for the dieter and the conscientious due to the oil used in cooking, is incredibly innocuous when air-popped. (Come to think of it, the same is true with oil-fried potatoes versus air-fried.) It's low in fat, high in fiber, and runs around 25 calories per filling, satisfying cup. (Please don't ask what to put on it. *Taste* the corn; don't just gulp it down. Soon a mouthful of buttered or salted popcorn will seem grossly cloying.)

Here's a final tip if you wake up in the middle of the night starving, but can't run any appliances or make any noise, lest you disturb others: Have a handful or two of your old-fashioned oats. Most people don't realize it, but they've already been steamed and are quite edible without any further cooking. They may taste a bit dry, but they'll fill you right up.

Of course, you could always eat cold cereal, but that's a topic for another chapter.

Vegetables

It seems odd to have a section on "vegetables," since they've been the main subject of the entire book. But that was in recipes in which they were combined with other ingredients in various fashions to produce main courses. Several dinners carried the suggestion to serve a vegetable on the side, and at lunch you may not want (or have time for) fancy preparations. So I'll give a few brief cooking hints to ensure that you get the same degree of gourmet flavor from your plain veggies as you do from elaborate concoctions, then conclude with one simple but elegant recipe that makes a scrumptious and visually stunning side dish.

Microwaving fresh and frozen vegetables is the best, because the brief cooking time and paucity of water used minimize the loss of flavor, nutrients, and textures. (Corn on the cob demonstrates this most dramatically, as I've argued so forcefully.) For frozen veggies, ignore the manufacturer's directions and don't add any water; the ice melting off the food will provide ample moisture. Put in an appropriate container, cover tightly with plastic wrap, poke a hole in the wrap with a fork, and cook on full power. One 10-ounce package takes 5-7 minutes, with thin

greens taking less time than denser items, such as Brussels sprouts. Stir one or more times during cooking. For "stalk" foods such as broccoli, it helps to cut it into pieces after it has cooked enough to be cut easily, and stir those pieces, lest the outside portions of the stalk get done before the middle, or the thinner florets get overdone. Check dish *before* you expect it to be done, and try to time it so it's done just as dinner is served—it will continue to cook as it sits.

Fresh vegetables are done the same way, except that you add about an ounce (2 tablespoons) of water for each half pound of food, and it takes a bit longer—7-8 minutes will do half a pound of green beans or asparagus just right for me. But make a note that extremely watery vegetables such as squash and zucchini, which produce much more steam and have much less "meat" to cook, take only about 5 minutes, and these two need no water added. (They also produce one of my favorite combinations. Mix slices of the two, in any proportion, and cook together for a colorful side dish at lunch or dinner.)

For stovetop cooking of fresh or frozen vegetables, either use a steamer basket, following manufacturer's instructions, or cook in the absolute least water required to prevent sticking, over low heat, tightly covered. This will give an effect somewhere between steaming and water-sautéing, rather than boiling, which you do *not* want. In fact, following the directions for the vegetables in pasta primavera (page 35), using a nonstick electric skillet or saucepan (and minus garlic, in most cases), should produce almost ideal results in just about any case.

Speaking of garlic, I don't add any seasonings to my vegetables when used as a side dish, rather than a main dish such as the primavera. I don't want them to compete with the flavor of the main dish, which is usually richly seasoned; I want to savor their own unique flavor, which will be different from the entree. Reread the comments on eggplant (page 50) and on sugar- and salt-sensitivity in the dessert chapter (pages 57, 58). Once you get used to the idea of *not* drowning your vegetables in butter, cream, salt, etc., you'll find that they do indeed have a taste of their own (often quite sweet, in the case of broccoli,

Brussels sprouts, and others) which is worth savoring for its unadorned self. Another reason you may not have appreciated these tastes all your life is overcooking, which was formerly endemic to American vegetable cookery but is fortunately on the decline, thanks to the interest in both gourmet cooking and nutrition. Canned vegetables of course, are by definition overcooked, due to the degree to which they are heated for sterilization during the canning process. Many an American developed a lifelong aversion to vegetables, remembered as tasteless and mushy, due to Mom's forcing him to eat canned green beans, lima beans, spinach, etc.

And now, having said all that, I'm going to give you a glorious exception—an easy-to-make side dish redolent with spices.

Broiled Tomatoes

These, if you recall, were heartily recommended with stuffed grape leaves (see page 53), but they contrast well with any other predominantly green dish or vegetable. They're also quite a contrast in themselves, in their Christmas red and green.

**Medium or larger ripe Beefsteak
    tomatoes
Garlic powder or, for a stronger taste,
    fresh crushed garlic
Onion powder
Basil
Oregano
Marjoram
Parsley flakes**

Line a baking sheet with aluminum foil, for easy cleanup. Cut tomatoes in half crosswise, i.e. at right angles to core. Scoop out seeds and juice. (I always save this and eat it later—pucker time!) Place halves face up on baking sheet. Sprinkle herbs and spices in juice hollows and over top until entire top surface has been covered with as much seasoning as it will hold. Broil on second-highest rack until juices are bubbling, spices are beginning to blacken at edges, edges are crinkly, and lower parts are beginning to wrinkle—about 10-15 minutes. Serve immediately. Wrap foil tightly over second helpings, shut off broiler, and keep in warm oven until needed. Leftovers should be tightly wrapped in plastic wrap and refrigerated and will reheat fairly satisfactorily in microwave or wrapped in foil in 350° oven.

Yield: As a side dish, allow 1 large tomato, 1-1 1/2 medium or 2 small tomatoes per person.

Variation: If you have large tomatoes with wide, deep seed pockets, you may fill them with crumbled cornbread (page 78) before adding spices.

Nutritional data: Based on medium (8-ounce) tomatoes.

PER HALF

Protein	1g
Carbohydrates	5g
Fat	0.2g
Calories	25
Fat by Calories	8.1%

This concludes our luncheon, bread, snack, and side-dish ideas. But there's still one meal left, isn't there?

6—L.C.

Chapter 11: Breakfast: Go With the Grain, Not Against It

Breakfast was served in the hotel dining room of a business convention I was attending. When my fairly typical breakfast order—four bowls of oatmeal—arrived, the conventioneer on my right turned and said, "Oh, do you always eat that much for breakfast?" Public discussions of how much I eat seem to be relatively common, as you saw in the lunch chapter. I know, and the commenters know, that it's rude to comment on another's eating habits, but I forgive them—most people *don't* understand how much low-fat food it takes to equal a small quantity of high-fat food, and besides, they're jealous.

Just as with my co-worker at lunch (page 65), I figured he'd asked for it. And the results came out about the same, too.

"If you look at the oatmeal," I said in a friendly tone, indicating that the question didn't surprise me, "you'll see that it has no butter, sugar, or cream, so the four servings total about 440 calories. You've got two eggs—that's about 110 calories, plus 100 or so for the butter used to fry them; three strips of bacon, at almost 200 calories a slice; around 200 calories worth of hash browns; and two pieces of toast—about 120 calories, and we'll be conservative and say you put only another tablespoon of butter on the two of them—so without even asking whether you put cream or sugar in your coffee, you're over 1,200 calories, plus your orange juice. Do you always eat that much for breakfast?"

He was taken properly aback at my reply. "I—I guess you're right," he stammered.

"But, yours just *looks* like a lot."

(Note: It wouldn't, if restaurants would quit serving such ridiculously small bowls of the stuff.) We had a brief conversation on the topic mentioned above, the relative calorie-density of high- and low-fat (and -sugar) foods—*very* brief, because I was hungry and my cereal was getting cold. I finished my oatmeal, and he his eggs.

It's probably just as well we didn't continue. He might have lost his appetite if he had found out that his breakfast contained over 100 grams of fat. (About as much as I eat in an entire *week* of breakfast, lunch, and dinner combined.) His breakfast also gave him well over 600 mg of cholesterol, which, again, is about as much as the body can safely process and excrete in the entire week, according to nonvegetarian, low-fat diets such as the Pritikin plan.

Yes, breakfast *is* another opportunity to get full and start the day well-fueled, on a surprisingly small amount of fat and calories (and zero cholesterol). And most people who have read anything at all on health know that bacon and eggs are out. But some of the proffered substitutes, by manufacturers ever eager to cash in on the latest bit of half-knowledge making the rounds (not to mention guilt and laziness), have a number of problems of their own. I'm not referring here to the self-deluders, who breakfast on croissants because they're advertised as "light." (The consumer thinks—or wants to think—that "light" means "light in calories." When the manufacturer says "light," it means "flaky." How do you make pastry flaky? You add more butter or shortening to it.) I'm referring to the latest marketing fad—the "adult" breakfast cereal.

Spurred by the conflict between our health-consciousness and our nostalgia for the chocolate-frosted sugar bombs on which we were reared in the 50s and 60s, scores of new cereals have been introduced, with words such as *fiber, bran,* and *granola* in their names. And I, for one, am grateful. They have turned label reading, normally a dull chore when buying bread, rolls, etc., into a delightful hobby. I love to wander the supermarkets and read the ingredients and analyses of these "healthful" cereals. They abound with high-fat ingredients such as almonds and other nuts, coconut, and oil with sawdust, or the equivalent thereof, added to support the "high-fiber" claim (and to dilute the calorie count of the fats). One brand pretends to be the cereal equivalent of a bran muffin—but who said commercial bran muffins were healthful, with their eggs, oil, and sweeteners? And the 4-inch long ingredient list has a lot of things that never found their way into Grandma's bran muffins.

These cereals are just as rich in sugars, though they disguise it in the same way salad dressings do (pages 75, 76)—by using smaller quantities of several different sweeteners. An example is a strawberry-flavored wheat biscuit. They start with whole wheat, then add three different kinds of sugar: corn syrup, sugar, and brown sugar—and then, finally, the strawberries. (No one ever told them that strawberries are naturally sweet.) If they used only one type of sugar, equaling the combined quantity of the three, it might very well outweigh wheat for first place on the ingredient list!

Fortunately for us, many cereals are now listing total sugar content as well as total carbohydrate content. (Carbohydrates include the starch or grains from which the cereal was made, plus the sugars.) These make really fun reading. Have a contest to see who can find the highest sugar figure—you'll probably have to go to the kiddie stuff to win this one. There are about 28 grams in an ounce, so when you see one which lists 14 grams of sugar per ounce (and there are many), it's half sugar. My record so far is 16!

Most of the adult cereals are not quite so high, partly because the fats have elbowed out some of the room for sugars in that ounce. Readings of six to eight grams per ounce are not uncommon, along with three to six grams of fat. (Beware of the "sweetened with fruit juice" ploy. Sugar is sugar, and some sweetened this way are among the highest in sugar content of the "healthful.") What *should* the figures be? Easy—zero for sugar, and the one to two grams of naturally occurring fats in an ounce of whole grains. (Those with zero fat are made from refined grains. See page 26.) But you don't have to read the analyses to determine this; just look at the ingredients. If it contains only grains, and nothing else, it matches these figures; if not, not. You will also generally find salt and an armload of chemicals included in the list. There is no need for any of these.

Salt for Breakfast

Speaking of salt, a statement has recently been circulated (I think by the potato-chip manufacturers) that Wheaties and Cheerios, ounce for ounce, have more sodium than potato chips. I don't eat either of these products, partly because of their added sugar and salt, but fair is fair, so I must come to their (partial) defense. Figures don't lie, as they say, but liars figure. Potato chips are fried in oil and pick up a good bit of this oil, so that one ounce of potato chips has a lot less "meat" (i.e. starch), than one ounce of cereal, and therefore needs, and has room for, less salt. The oil also gives them about one-third more calories per ounce than the cereal, with a fat-to-total-calories ratio of about 50 percent, compared to around 10 percent for the cereal. If I were sentenced to live off of only one of these foods forever, I'd go with the cereal. End of defense.

Hot Cereal

My favorite breakfast, as the chapter opening implied. Hot cereals are not only more satisfying and filling than cold, they're also generally less refined (don't eat the refined versions, such as Cream of Wheat and Cream of Rice, more apt to be available as plain grains, unadulterated by sweeteners, salt, or fat, and don't require the preservatives of the more heavily milled and cooked cold cereals. They're a great way to start the day in any but the hottest weather—and when I lived in the subtropical swamps, the omnipresent super-airconditioning made them attractive then too. (Incidentally, they're also cheaper than processed cereals, naturally enough; you can fill up for perhaps ten or fifteen cents a day.)

BUT I DON'T HAVE TIME IN THE MORNING TO MAKE A HOT BREAKFAST!

And you probably think I'm going to tell you to get up ten minutes earlier. Wrong. (I like to sleep as much as anyone else.) Instead I'm going to show you that it takes no longer to fix a hot breakfast than to fix a cold one or a cup of coffee, and certainly less time than bacon and eggs.

Run the tap water hot while you measure desired quantity of cereal into appropriately-sized saucepan. (If you have an electric range, turn burner on "high" before you do these, since it takes time to heat up.) Add water. Stir and place on high heat (or however hot your burner has gotten by now). Bring to boil, stirring occasionally. Total time so far is about three to five minutes. Reduce heat to simmer and cook until not quite thick enough, stirring frequently—from one to five minutes. (The package directions will be a guideline, but only that. *You* decide how thick you like your cereal.) Turn off heat (and remove saucepan from electric burner) and cover tightly. Now go do something else—shower, shave, get dressed, whatever—for anywhere from two to ten minutes; pick a chore that fits this time frame conveniently. Come back, stir cereal, empty into bowl, fill pot with cold water (for easier cleanup later), and eat. Total time spent cooking: as little as four minutes, and certainly not over ten. (If you're in a *real* rush and like the longer-cooking cereals, do a longer chore during sitting time so you have to cook cereal for a shorter time. It gets thicker and more done the longer it sits.) If you're genuinely compulsive and can't stand eating slowly, do something else useful while it sits in your bowl until it's cool enough to wolf down.

What if you have more time? Most hot cereals develop an even better flavor if cooked a little longer, but more water must be added to keep them from getting too thick. In fact, the manufacturer's directions for quantity of water should be taken only as a starting point, just as recipe suggestions for spicing. I like my cereals a little thinner than called for by the directions; others prefer a thick porridge which they can "sink their teeth into." Let the recipe be a minimum amount of water to use; if you want it thicker, cook longer; if thinner, or if you wish to cook longer for flavor (or both), add more water.

What to add to your cereal? Well, we certainly didn't go through that long discussion of verboten ingredients in prepackaged cereals just to add the same things to our homemade, did we? Naturally, we're not going to add salt to the cooking water (or afterward), no matter *what* the box says. (It'll cook fine without it. Trust me.) Ditto sugar, honey, molasses, etc.

What then? For me personally, nothing, just like my vegetables (page 80). Yes, here we go again, with the same discussion of increased sugar- and salt-sensitivity as on pages 57, 58. (Reread it and save me the trouble of rewriting it.) It's true, though; my friend Ruth weaned herself down from sweeter cold cereals to Cheerios, about the lowest-sugar presweetened cereal around, but after six months or so she began to complain of the sugar (and salty!) taste of those and finally switched to the sugar- and salt-free version (of which we'll hear shortly). Grains *do* have taste, just like eggplant.

Natural Sweeteners

I realize, though, that the weaning period can be disconcerting, especially if you were accustomed to butter and sugar on hot cereals, or to even sweeter breakfasts, such as d**ghn*ts, or whatever. So, for the sweet tooth, sprinkle sliced banana over cooked cereal, or fresh or frozen fruit such as strawberries, blueberries, raspberries, and the like. (The heat from the cereal should thaw them quickly, if frozen; if not, or if this cools the cereal too much for you, add frozen fruit while cereal cooks or sits covered. But try not to overcook fruit.) Fresh apple slices (peeled, if you like) will give one taste if added to finished product, a different taste if cooked in with cereal from the start. Any of these, or any combination thereof, should add plenty of "sweet" without the need for honey, fruit juice, etc. Or, as an alternative, sprinkle cinnamon over hot cereal or during cooking. For really desperate cases, use fruit *and* cinnamon. Eventually, you may wish to reduce gradually the quantity of fruit; in any event, you're much better off than with virtually any processed cereal.

Now for the good news. You don't even have to make a trip to the health-food store to acquire this bounty. My favorite is good old Quaker oats, right there on the same supermarket shelf where it's been for two-hundred years or so, at less than a nickel an ounce in the jumbo box, which I go through pretty quickly. You'll also find Wheatena, which has the strong, nutty flavor of roasted wheat, and (probably in kosher foods, not in cereals) buckwheat, to which you were introduced as a type of spaghetti. The buckwheat kernels, known as kasha, are sold as a grain or vegetable dish but make a better cereal, in my opinion. They are available in coarse, medium, and fine grain, to suit your preference for consistency, and have an even stronger flavor than Wheatena. Both should silence anyone who complains that plain oatmeal is too bland.

Your supermarket will also have cornmeal and probably corn grits, unless you live several thousand miles from the Mason-Dixon line. Grits are popular as a vegetable or side dish in the South, served with gravy; they make a fine breakfast just as they are. Plain cornmeal, as used in cornbread (page 78) can also be used as a breakfast cereal. Use 4-5 parts water to 1 part cornmeal, and cook a bit longer than for most cereals. (Ignore anything you may have read concerning the need for a double boiler. Just keep turning the heat lower and lower as it thickens.) These two products are more refined than the others mentioned (which also accounts for their lower fat and calorie count); try to buy yellow instead of white for the same reasons as you bought yellow corn (page 64). I don't eat this when my lunch corn is in season!

Other items you may find in your supermarket (or natural-foods store), are Oat Bran and rolled Whole Wheat hot cereal, both sold under the labels of either Quaker or Mother's (same company). The oat bran has a different flavor and a creamier, grainier texture than rolled oats (oatmeal); the wheat flakes have not been preroasted and are milder than Wheatena. Both are

super-quick cooking, requiring only one or two minutes after boiling; be sure to increase the water if you wish to cook them longer. (Now that we've mentioned adding fruit, another reason for cooking cereal longer than minimum time is to allow, say, apples to cooking longer in it.)

How much more selection you have without making a trip to the health-food house depends on your supermarket. Some have expanded their cereal sections to include a considerable number of items formerly found only in health-food stores, or have a separate natural-foods section which contains them. Others carry very little which isn't junk. Assume that the remainder of the suggested cereals are health-store items; if your supermarket stocks them, you've found a good supermarket.

Cream of Rye is the rye equivalent of the rolled Whole Wheat cereal—grains of rye steamed and rolled to be quick-cooking (though not as quick as wheat). Despite the name similarity to Cream of Wheat, it has not been refined, as has the latter, which is made from white-flour-type refined wheat. It has quite a chewy texture and a flavor whose strength is somewhere between that of hot whole wheat and the toasted Wheatena. It's a real change, too, because oats, wheat, and corn are all familiar to us from our cold-cereal days (however disguised they were), whereas rye is not. Try it.

Steel-cut Nuggets

Steel-cut oats are for weekends. Uncooked whole oats, instead of being steamed and rolled as for oatmeal, are merely cut into smaller chunks, so they take about 20-25 minutes to cook. They remain as distinct nuggets with a delightfully chewy texture, and so make a pleasant variation from oatmeal (or satisfy those who feel that the latter is too gruellike in consistency).

By the way, while we're on the subject of oats, rye, and wheat, the original berries of all three of these can also be made into breakfast cereals. (Remember wheat and rye berries from the lunch chapter? Whole oat berries, called groats, are on the same shelf.) Put a cup of any one into a slow cooker with 5 cups of water and simmer overnight. You will awaken to a fragrant kitchen and to soft, chewy morsels in a thick sauce. If you want my opinion (which is why you bought the book), it's not worth the trouble, especially the cleanup, but it does save cooking time on those busy mornings. See for yourself if you like it enough to bother.

Elam's makes a product called Scotch oatmeal, which is basically whole oats ground almost to an oat flour. Be careful—several other manufacturers use the term Scotch to refer to steel-cut oats. This grind is rather quick-cooking and creamy like Oat Bran but milder in flavor. It also thickens very quickly once it "sets," and while it sits, so watch closely; vigorous and frequent stirring is also necessary to prevent lumping. On the other hand, a thoroughly-cooked lump can provide some texture, just as in mashed potatoes.

Multigrain combinations are very popular in natural-food stores, such as 4-grain, 7-grain, etc. These usually consist of some combination of wheat, rye, barley, corn, oats, millet, and perhaps buckwheat, rice, and a little flaxseed thrown in for "crunch." Many people enjoy having such a variety of flavors and textures in one bowl. Experiment to see which ones you like. Don't be afraid to waste a dollar or two if you don't like one—the birds will thank you for them.

Many other hot cereals, such as brown rice cereal await your browsing the aisles of your purveyor of goodies. In fact, you're liable to see new ones each time you shop. Just check the labels, and if they consist only of whole grains, without added fats, sugars, or salt, try whichever look appealing. If in doubt about what has been added, look for no more than two grams of fat per ounce, or per 100 calories if the serving quoted is other than one ounce.

Speaking of nutritive data, most plain whole grains, such as those listed above, will be similar in the vital statistics. One ounce will provide 100-110 calories (except for the more refined grits, which run about 80) and around one gram of fat for all except the oat products, which have two. Protein content varies from two to six grams, but you know better than to worry about that; the rest of the calories will be supplied by carbohydrate (starch, not sugar!).

A question occasionally arises when the manufacturer has failed to specify just how much cereal weighs one ounce (the typical, standard "serving.") Figure three ounces per cup of oatmeal, oat bran and whole wheat cereal; four ounces per cup of corn grits, Elam's Scotch oats and Cream of Rye; five for Wheatena, and six for cornmeal, buckwheat, and steel-cut oats (and for the whole grain berries). You can see that you might end up hungry, or with leftovers, if you always used the same quantity of dry cereal and then tried a different variety. (Note: Left-over cereals do not reheat at all well, in microwave, or stove, or over campfire. They turn into a gummy mess. Throw them out or mail them to the starving people overseas.)

This brings up yield information. One ounce is a convenient measure for the manufacturers; how much do real people eat? Obviously, you'll find out soon enough, in your own case; if you're trying a new one, just eat as many ounces (or calories' worth, if they differ markedly in calories per ounce) as you do of a familiar cereal. Equally obvious, this will depend not only on your general appetite but on whether you plan to run a marathon later in the morning, but here are a few guidelines, anyway.

Two ounces usually takes care of the modest to average appetite of a not too active individual; figure three ounces for the more active, physically larger, or hungrier person; four ounces for the very active or voracious eaters. Don't be bashful about eating more, if you need it; when I used to run six to ten miles daily (instead of my current three to six), I ate five ounces of cereal at breakfast and was plenty hungry for lunch four hours later. You'll be filling your energy needs with good, complex carbohydrates with lots of fiber and taking in quite a bit of water at the same time to prevent dehydration during exercise. (I've hardly had a glass of water, or any other beverage, with meals in two years. But that's another story, and one that most people refuse to believe.)

Roll Your Own

Would you like to be absolutely sure that your cereal is the pure, unadulterated stuff, and save money in the process? Well, as the old saying goes, if you want something done right, do it yourself. Here's how to make a quick-cooking hot cereal from raw ingredients at home.

Place 1/2 cup of whole brown rice, wheat berries, or rye berries in a blender. Blend at low speed for a couple of minutes, stopping once to shake the jar so the unblended ones get down to the blades. Speed up the blender the last 30 seconds or so. Transfer to saucepan, add 2 1/4 - 2 1/2 cups water, bring to a boil, reduce heat, and simmer uncovered, stirring frequently, until rather less done than desired. This will take 5-10 minutes for rice, 10-15 for wheat or rye. Cover and remove from heat. Let sit for *at least* 5 minutes; longer is better. Stir and serve. Makes a 300 calorie serving; for a larger, 400 calorie serving (or two smaller portions at 200 each), use 2/3 cup of grain and 3 cups water. Note: if time is a real factor, blend the night before and store overnight in a plastic bag. I'd be reluctant to make larger quantities, though, since once the grains are broken up and their protective shells are breached, they won't keep as well without the dreaded preservatives.

The Thrifty Vegetarian

I stumbled on this idea after trying a hot cereal sold in my friendly local health-food store. The only ingredient listed was brown rice, so I tried it and liked it. But it occurred to me that it looked very much like rice which had simply been broken up in a mill or blender, packed in airtight cellophane single-serving packets due to the problem described above. It was about two and a half dollars per pound. With whole brown rice retailing for 32¢-44¢ per pound, it didn't take me long to figure out that I was paying someone over $2 a pound to put my rice through a blender! I determined to try it myself. The rest, as they say, is history.

Incidentally, you can make a super-convenience hot cereal in the same manner by using any of the acceptable cold cereals discussed in the next section. First find out how much cold cereal equals one ounce—it may vary from as little as 2/3 cup (Shredded Wheat) to 2 cups (puffed corn or millet). If the package doesn't say, you'll have to weigh it. Add one cup of water for each ounce of cereal (that's why you had to weigh it; measuring the cereals by volume would produce drastically different results for each cereal, since the different processing methods inflate the grains by different amounts). Cook as above; most take only 5 minutes. Especially good candidates for this

treatment are wheat flakes, corn flakes, and Shredded Wheat.

Speaking of cold cereals, let's take a look at them. I promise it'll be interesting!

Cold Cereals

If you played the label game diligently and were in a typical supermarket, you found exactly one survivor: Shredded Wheat, and one or two imitators, perhaps. The only listed ingredient is 100 percent whole wheat. The manufacturer even put the preservatives into the bag material instead of into the cereal. Grape Nuts comes close enough; the barley malt added leaves it quite low in total sugar. But beware of Grape Nuts Flakes with raisins in them (or any other cereal which contains raisins or other dried fruit). Raisins, and all dried fruits, are incredibly high in sugar in relation to their bulk because of the loss of filling water. Another tricky example of the "hidden sugar" game!

Does this mean that you're limited to one or two cold cereals the rest of your life? Hardly. Put your browsing sneakers back on and head to your natural-foods store. In their cereal aisle, you can play the label game with the hope of finding frequent winners, rather than for the sake of sneering at the losers. Remember, though, that the fact that they are sold in a different type of store or are made by smaller companies is no guarantee that all of the cereals therein will be healthful. Many people still cling to the nuts-and-granola-are-good-for-you school of health food, and whether the well-meaning manufacturer suffers from the same delusion or simply tries to fulfill perceived demand at profit (a laudable motive), the result is the same.

Once you weed out the ones with added fats and sugars, your remaining choices will be far larger than they were at the supermarket. In fact, the very first items to look at, to help make the transition and sort of get you in the mood, are the clean-up versions of major manufacturers' cereals. You will find NatureOs, Oatios, or other brands of oat cereal, which are essentially Cheerios minus the sugar and salt. (Wait a minute, we've got this backward again. Cheerios is a basically healthful oat cereal which has then had sugar and salt added to it.) There is puffed corn, which is what Trix and Sugar Pops were before they mixed them 50/50 with sugar and added the food colorings. Puffed rice and puffed wheat are already familiar as major brand cereals under those names. Here, however, all three are "single ingredient" cereals, with a list of ingredients consisting of exactly corn or wheat or rice. (Speaking of puffed wheat, when I was a kid there was a sweetened puffed wheat cereal called Super Sugar Crisp. There was a big flap over the amount of sugar in children's breakfast cereals. So the manufacturer did the responsible thing. He changed the name to Super Golden Crisp.

You will also find single-ingredient wheat flakes and corn flakes, for a sugar- and salt-free "breakfast of champions" or for nostalgia for our most popular kiddie cereal. (Remember that the corn flour has been degermed and so is more refined than the whole grains used in the wheat, rice, and oat cereals.)

Other qualifying cereals, rather than being pure versions of commercially popular cereals, are originals. Puffed millet is an example. It's practically all air—it takes about thirty-six boxes to make an ounce of the stuff—so it's a great psychological boost for dieters who want to see that they're eating a *lot*. Like its regular cooked counterpart, to which you were introduced in the chapter on Mexican cooking, it has a very mild flavor, so is especially suitable for mixing with other cereals.

The Bikini Principle

Incidentally, when you hit the checkout stand, expect to encounter the women's-bikini principle here too; the less material that goes into something, the more it costs. Yes, it *should* cost less to produce a cereal when you don't have to add sweeteners, salt, and chemicals to it, or amortize the cost of General Mills' or Kellogg's advertising budget, but these manufacturers are producing in much smaller volumes and because of the lack of preservatives they also must store and ship smaller quantities to your store, which cannot buy in bulk for the same reason. (On the topic of shelf life, I find that preservative-free cereals still keep rather well in their sealed packages—and many of them are packaged much better than com-

mercial cereals, in thicker paper or even aluminum foil—but once opened, they will not stay fresh nearly so long as the chemical concoctions will. That's probably why they are usually sold in smaller boxes.)

Continuing to browse, you will discover that you can expand your range even further if you decide that you wish to tolerate small quantities of malt, fruit, juice, or salt. The quantity varies considerably, so you may find you like some but find others too sweet. My Geiger-counterlike sugar-detecting tongue does not care for these at all; if you'd like just a trace, take a tip from helpmate Ruth and mix some of a sweetened cereal into a bowl of the unadulterated stuff. For that matter, mix *any* two (or three or seven) cereals that you like, regardless of sweeteners or lack of same. Especially good are combinations of an airy, puffed cereal or a light, flaky one with a dense cereal such as Grape Nuts. And finally, an excellent use for a malt- or juice-sweetened cereal is as topping for Apple Crisp, page 59.

Examples of these cereals are Crispy Oats and Oat Bran Crunch, dense, crunchy nuggets of oats or oat bran, brown-rice flour, and malt; various flakes of bran, oats, amaranth, and a *nine*-grain combination (wheat, bran, oat bran, oats, barley, rye, buckwheat, amaranth, and corn); and Nutty Rice, very dense, crunchy rice nuggets with raisin sweetener and, inexplicably, sea salt (who cares where the salt came from?). This last is definitely a mixing candidate, and probably a good one after which to draw the line, even though, at 80mg sodium per ounce, it's labeled "low sodium." Go beyond this, ingredient-wise, and we're back into the same fat, sugar, and salt routine as with the commercial "adult" cereals, although the sweeteners will be labeled brown sugar, honey, dried fruit, etc., and the fats will appear in impressive-sounding guises too.

And now for the question that's been in the back of your mind the entire time: What does a vegetarian put on cold cereal, if not milk? I have read suggestions to use either water or fruit juice and do not care for either (and wouldn't use high-sugar fruit juice anyway). My answer is, My hands (or a spoon, if someone is looking). This is just like the bottled-salad-dressing question on page 76: Just because you've always poured something on cereal doesn't mean that you always have to. Look at it this way: You don't pour milk, or anything else, on bread, crackers, bagels, or other baked-grain products, do you? So why do you have to pour it on these perfectly nutritious baked-grain cereals? You pick up a whole-wheat matzo right out of the box and eat it, right? Why not do the same with your cereal?

BUT IT WON'T SEEM LIKE BREAK-FAST!

For once, I agree. With or without milk, or whatever, cold cereals *aren't* as filling and satisfying as hot cereals, which contain much more water (when cooked) and have more natural fiber due to being less processed. That's one reason why I said that they weren't my breakfast recommendation. But this "method" makes them ideally suited for three purposes:

(1) If you oversleep, for example, and *really* don't have time to fix or eat breakfast. Grab a box or two of cereal as you fly out the door and munch on the bus or train, at stoplights, or when you get to work.

(2) As emergency food, kept in reserve. If your work is of the type which occasionally (or often) delays or even precludes meal breaks, a box of cereal stashed away can keep you going. Just knowing that it's there, in fact, will often help you continue working even if you don't need it—there's nothing like not being able to eat to make you hungry!

Less of an emergency, but also a useful application, is car trips, where you may not be sure when, or where, you will be able to stop to eat or what they will have to offer when you do. Your stash can keep you from being forced into eating something you don't want to, or shouldn't. This is even more applicable on airplane trips—I always pack a box to protect myself in case the airline "vegetarian" meal is less than expected and to prevent the extremely desperate situation of having to eat in an airport. And it certainly doesn't hurt to have a good cold cereal sitting in a motel room, where the local cuisine may be an unknown quantity. (On week-long vacations, I pack a hot plate, hot cereal, and one pot. But then, cold cereal doesn't seem as appetizing at a ski resort.)

Note: Use the smallest box available for these purposes, and once opened, rotate it into your regular stock if you do not finish it

shortly, bringing a new box to replenish your hoard at work or wherever. See page 76 about lack of preservatives.

(3) Best use of all, in my opinion, for cold cereals—as snacks. At any time, day, evening, or middle of the night, a tasty, crunchy, filling cereal can fill that empty spot in your life as nothing else can. Easy to fix, no leftover problem, and always available—what could be better? Keep a variety on hand.

But what else to have for breakfast, in place of (or in addition to, for you marathoners) hot cereal, either for a change or when in a rush? Look again at the section on breads (pages 77-80). Homemade cornbread or oatmeal bread, bagels, or your favorite, carefully-screened health-food store bread can be eaten fresh or popped in the microwave or toaster if frozen.

Happy Travels

I hope you've enjoyed our trip through the tasty, healthful world of low-fat vegetarian cooking, and I hope I've put to rest any misconceptions you may have had about vegetarian cuisine or nutritional adequacy. Let me know which recipes you especially like and which you didn't like or had problems with; perhaps I can help with the latter. If there are any particular types of recipes which you'd like to see developed in the future, please let me know that also; I'm always experimenting and adding new stock to my repertoire. Perhaps I can give you some suggestions on how to adapt your favorite existing recipes to meet the dietary guidelines followed in this book. For that matter, if you have any gems which already meet the guidelines which you'd like to share with the world, please pass them along! (Write to me in care of the publisher. Don't forget to include a stamped, self-addressed envelope with any correspondence.)

In my opinion, every reader of this book deserves a great deal of credit simply for being willing to listen to suggestions which go against a lifetime of habit. I hope, as your reward, that you've had as much enjoyment from eating these recipes as I've had from producing them.

Yours in happiness, health, and long life.

Steve Victor

Postscript

Protein Paranoia (and Calcium Qualms)

It was around the eighth mile of a 30 kilometer (18.6 mile) race. I had fallen in step with two other runners who were cruising along at the same eight-minutes-per-mile pace I was, none of us "racing" in the sense of being in an extreme hurry, but simply looking forward to the pride of having completed such a distance. Total strangers an hour ago, we had become friends through the common bond of the effort we shared in pursuing our goal, as often happens during such events.

As equally often happens, the talk turned to training methods and, thereby, to diet. (Not at my initiative—as I mentioned, I don't proselytize.) I related that a major improvement in my training—to the tune of about 30 seconds per mile—had occurred within a few months of my adopting a low-fat vegetarian lifestyle.

"You don't eat any meat at all?" asked a companion, interested. (Runners are as interested in improving their times as the rest of the world is in losing weight.)

"Haven't in a year," I replied.

"Oh," He pondered. "You eat a lot of chicken and fish, then, huh?"

This question always puzzles me. I have always considered chickens and red snappers as being animals, rather than vegetables. However, the question was a common one; in fact, the entire conversation, I knew, would be a replay of a well-worn script. I got ready to play the elimination game.

"No," I answered, "I don't eat any animal products at all."

"Oh." He pondered deeper. "Do you eat eggs?"

"Nope."

"What about dairy products?"

"Unh-unh."

He diverted his attention from the road ahead long enough to look over at me, apparently observing that I was running as well as he was and appeared to be reasonably healthy, or at least in no imminent danger of collapsing. He thought some more; I waited.

"Do you eat a lot of nuts?" he finally asked.

"Never," I replied. "Much too fatty."

"Well, then," his exasperation was breaking through. "What DO you eat?"

"Let's see," I thought out loud. "Last night I had spaghetti, and Friday I had chow mein, and the night before that was, I think, burritos. . . ." I explained to him what I said in an earlier chapter about the huge array of vegetables and grains that grew on this earth and the varied assortment of dishes I can fashion from them.

His interest returned, relieved that I was not propounding a steady diet of potatoes three times a day. But I knew this act had one more scene before the curtain.

"Do you eat a lot of beans?" he inquired.

"Not a lot," I answered. "On the average, about once a week, I guess, in stuff such as the burritos."

"But where do you get your protein!?!"

At last it was out—the question that comes at the end of virtually every such discussion I have had, occasionally accompanied, if the asker is somewhat sophisticated nutritionally, by, "Do you practice food balancing?"—or matching or combining or some such.

This is what I refer to as "protein paranoia"—the nearly universal belief that everyone in this country is constantly tottering on the brink of some horrible protein deficiency, and that all of us—especially vegetarians—must carefully sit down and plot each day's food intake to make sure of getting enough of eight or nine different amino acids to avoid unnamed but catastrophic consequences, such as, I suppose, imploding like a broken television tube.

Health Food Scare

Unfortunately, this belief seems to be most strongly held by the legion of "health writers" in the popular media, who simultaneously urge us to reduce fat and cholesterol intake and scare us away from taking exactly those steps that would best accomplish this. In fact, the worst offenders are often the "vegetarian" cookbook authors themselves. One not at all atypical example contains over 1,300 meatless recipes, some of which may indeed serve as starting points to inspire the creation of true vegetarian dishes. But shortly after the authors tell us that Americans consume too much protein, they give us four pages admitting the alleged "inferiority" of vegetable protein to animal protein and explaining the "necessity" of combining certain foods with others at the same meal, lest the proteins in the individual foods slide through unused, completely wasted. (Don't you wish calories would do the same thing?) Included, of course, is the de rigueur chart of what to combine with what—e.g. beans with rice, nuts with cheese, etc. As a result of this philosophy, most of the main-dish recipes in that particular book contain eggs, cheese, or milk; those which do not, suffer the indignity of being labeled "Minor Protein," along with an admonition to serve them with a side dish containing one or more of these animal foods. So much for reducing fat, cholesterol, and calories!

The truth of the matter, of course, is that, as with almost every other nutrient, the problem with protein in the American diet is one of excess, not deficiency. But before covering this issue I would like to make two things, as they say, perfectly clear.

(1) The purpose of this book is *not* to convince you to become vegetarian or to give you medical reasons for doing so. Its purpose is to give you recipes should you decide on your own to do so, as I did.

(2) I am *not* a doctor or medical researcher. I am, at the moment, a cookbook writer.

My own dietary philosophy, however, *was* evolved after a considerable amount of reading works by those who *are* doctors or medical researchers. To my mind, two authors, and two books in particular, stand out in this field, in presenting lucid, compelling reasons for altering one's eating habits, complete with footnotes of exhaustive medical studies documenting virtually very statement made. They are (1) *The Pritikin Promise: 28 Days to a Longer, Healthier Life,* by the late Nathan Pritikin[1], and (2) *The McDougall Plan*, by John A. McDougall, M.D. and Mary A. McDougall.[2] I recommend both highly. (Please note that the Pritikin program is not vegetarian, even in the lacto-ovo sense; small amounts of lean flesh are permitted. But the book's explanations of the consequences of excessive intake of fat, cholesterol, and protein make a compelling case for the adoption of an extremely low-fat, low- (if not zero) cholesterol, low-protein diet.)

Why, then, am I even addressing the issue? Because I fear that otherwise some readers, who have a preconception of what "vegetarian" eating should be like, may be puzzled when they see the recipes, and perhaps fear to try them, or even worse "supplement" them with "high-protein" ingredients. So what I shall do is merely make a few statements to counter whatever myths you may have heard and make reference to the pertinent parts of the above two books should you wish to read a fuller explanation

1. New York: Simon and Schuster, 1983.
2. Piscataway, N.J.: New Century Publishers, Inc., 1983.

and/or see the supporting documentation.

But first, back to my friend, the runner. (We're probably at mile nine by now—time flies when you're having an interesting discussion.) He had asked where I got my protein.

"From everything I eat," I told him. "Every living, growing thing has protein, whether animal or vegetable, or it wouldn't live. Rice has protein. Potatoes have protein. Even lettuce has protein."

"Lettuce?"

Yes, even lettuce, I explained. In fact, over 33 percent of the calories in lettuce come from protein. If you eat 2,000 calories a day, and if you ate them in the form of nothing but lettuce, you would get about 170 grams of protein—more than double what even the high-protein fanatics would have you eat and about five or six times what you actually need. By contrast, if you obtained your daily caloric need from nothing but boneless sirloin steak, you would take in only 98 grams of protein! So much for your childhood (and current) teaching that certain foods are "protein foods," as though they were the only ones that contained protein and all others did not!

The problem, of course, is that it is very difficult to eat 2,000 calories worth of lettuce. Unlike steak, lettuce is high in non-caloric fiber and is about 95 percent water, so that you would have to eat over 50 pounds of the stuff to meet your needs. You'd burst first.

Protein Everywhere

Still, the point is the same. Every whole, unrefined fruit, vegetable, and grain that you eat is contributing protein to your diet, not just certain foods such as beans. (Obviously, though, you're going to eat some denser foods, such as rice and potatoes, not just lettuce!)

ISN'T IT EVER POSSIBLE NOT TO GET ENOUGH PROTEIN?

Yes, of course. Suppose you decided to meet your assumed 2,000 calorie daily need by drinking eleven or so 16-ounce colas. You would indeed obtain 2,000 calories (burp!). And you would obtain zero protein. (You'd also obtain zero fat, although this type of low-fat diet is hardly recommended!) The

reason, of course, is that the only "nutrient" in the cola is sugar, and sugar isn't a vegetable, it's *part* of a vegetable. When they took out the sugar to give you, they threw away, or gave to some other lucky person or animal, the rest of the beet—and whole beets are about 15 percent protein, calorically. And you could achieve the same result, with perhaps more short-term fun but even quicker grave consequences, by drinking 2,000 calories worth of alcohol—another distilled, refined fragment of a grain. The point is, this can't happen if the bulk of your diet is made up of unrefined, whole grains and vegetables instead of highly processed food fragments such as sugar and alcohol.

SO, HOW DO I MAKE SURE I GET ENOUGH PROTEIN?

Every day, you face starvation if you fail to eat enough food to meet your body's needs. How do you avoid starving?

THAT'S SILLY. IF I DON'T EAT ENOUGH I GET HUNGRY.

Bingo! Eat enough nonjunk food every day to avoid starvation and hunger, and you'll automatically get enough protein.

BUT I WAS IN THE GYM THE OTHER DAY, AND THERE WAS A BIG CHART ON THE WALL SHOWING HOW SOME PLANT FOODS WERE DEFICIENT IN CERTAIN AMINO ACIDS AND OTHERS WERE HIGH IN THEM, AND TO MIX AND MATCH CAREFULLY IF I DIDN'T WANT TO EAT "COMPLETE" PROTEINS SUCH AS MILK, EGGS, AND MEAT.

I don't suppose there was also a bottle of amino acid capsules for sale at the front desk?

YES, NOW THAT YOU MENTION IT. BUT WHAT ABOUT THAT CHART IN THE COOKBOOK YOU MENTIONED EARLIER? THEY WEREN'T SELLING ANYTHING.

Sigh. OK, here goes.

1. Every plant food contains every amino acid—McDougall, page 98.

2. While the proportions of the acids in each food vary, eating any of them, or any combination thereof, in amounts adequate to meet daily calorie needs, will provide enough of each amino acid—McDougall, page 99.

3. The studies of proteins and amino acid requirements relied upon by the charts, cookbooks, and, in fact, virtually every food writer today (often unaware that they are

relying on them) were done on *rats,* not humans. Rats are a fairly good substitute for humans in some studies—say, perhaps, cancer—but a rat's proportionate need for protein is demonstrably greater than a human's—Pritikin, page 384; McDougall, Page 96, chart page 101.

4. No one has been able to produce, or find a case of, an actual *protein* deficiency in an otherwise normal human being. Those who are cited as such (say, in the Ethiopia famine) are actually victims of *food* deficiency, i.e. starvation. They don't need us to send them "high-protein" foods or develop "winged beans" with more protein than regular beans—they just need *more to eat* of the same basic grains and vegetables they're already accustomed to consuming—Pritikin, page 386; McDougall, page 100.

5. Excessive protein intake is actually *harmful* to your kidneys and has other side effects, as we'll see in a minute—McDougall, pages 102-104; Pritikin, pages 391, 392. So quit worrying about getting enough amino acids and just eat.

WHAT TIME OF DAY SHOULD I EAT, AND HOW OFTEN?

When you're hungry.

I CAN'T BELIEVE IT. IT SOUNDS TOO SIMPLE.

Did you, or the protein writers, ever stop to think that people of thousands of years ago had no pocket calculators (and couldn't have found batteries for it if they had), and certainly didn't sit down and calculate each day's assortment of nutrients? They didn't even know which amino acids were in which food, but they didn't starve and thereby "extinct" the human race. Quit calculating and start cooking.

GREAT! SO WHY DO ALL THESE WRITERS STILL BELIEVE IN THE FOOD-COMBINING BUSINESS?

One reason is that no one has told them differently. Another is that many people keep telling them the same—people with a vested interest in doing so.

YOU MEAN AMINO-ACID SALESMEN? I DON'T PAY ANY ATTENTION TO THEM.

No, I mean beef salesman, egg salesmen, and milk-and-cheese salesmen.

HEY, WAIT A MINUTE. NOW THAT YOU MENTION IT, THE DAIRY PEOPLE ARE PUSHING PRETTY HARD LATELY, BUT IT'S NOT FOR AMINO ACIDS. IT'S FOR CALCIUM. WHAT AM I GOING TO DO FOR CALCIUM, WITHOUT MILK AND CHEESE?

All right, now you've done it. We're going to have a pop quiz. Take out a sheet of paper and number from one to three.

Ready? OK, question one: Which has more calcium, an eight-ounce serving of fresh broccoli or eight ounces of cottage cheese?

WELL, OBVIOUSLY THE CHEESE, RIGHT?

Wrong. The broccoli has 233 milligrams of calcium; the cottage cheese, 213 milligrams.

REALLY. OK, BUT THE NEWSPAPER ARTICLES ARE TELLING ME TO EAT *LOW FAT* DAIRY FOODS, SUCH AS SKIM MILK, TO GET A LOT OF CALCIUM HEALTHFULLY.

Let's see. Question two: Which has more calcium, a 100-calorie serving of fresh, cooked broccoli, or a 100-calorie glass of skim milk?

I'M INCLINED TO SAY THE MILK, BUT I'VE GOT THE SINKING FEELING THAT IF IT WERE YOU WOULDN'T HAVE ASKED THE QUESTION.

You're catching on. The broccoli wins by a nose, 338 milligrams to 336 milligrams.

WAIT A MINUTE; THAT'S A TRICK QUESTION—JUST LIKE THE PROTEIN IN THE LETTUCE. THE BROCCOLI HAS LOTS OF FIBER AND WATER, UNLIKE THE MILK, WHICH IS FULL OF PROTEIN.

Sounds to me like a good argument for preferring the broccoli, doesn't it? But we'll play it your way for question three: Which has more calcium, eight ounces of fresh broccoli or eight ounces of milk?

LET ME GUESS—THE BROCCOLI, RIGHT?

Today just isn't your day. In fact, the milk finally wins one—274 milligrams to 233. But I gave the milk people easy competition—eight ounces of raw mustard greens has 415 milligrams of calcium! Boiling them in water reduces this to 313—still well above the milk, and you could probably cut the loss by microwaving it instead of boiling it. But even these figures pale before the mighty collard green—567 milligrams of calcium in eight ounces, more than twice that of skim milk! Even after cooking, it retains 426 milligrams.

The point isn't which foods have the most

calcium. The point is that, just as the protein pushers tried to give you the idea that only animal foods were good protein sources, and vegetable foods had little or no protein (of "inferior quality"), the dairy people are trying to create the impression that dairy foods are the only reasonable source of adequate calcium. As you have seen, they are not.

BUT THEY TELL ME THAT IT'S HARD TO GET ENOUGH CALCIUM, EVEN WITH DAIRY PRODUCTS. IN FACT, THEY NOW HAVE MILK FORTIFIED WITH EXTRA CALCIUM.

Isn't that disgusting? Especially when you consider that too much calcium, just like too much protein, is bad for you, that the end result of all the dairy products and oyster-shell tablets being consumed these days (mostly by women) will be a vast increase in the number of kidney stones—McDougall, pages 53, 102.

BAD FOR YOU? THEN HOW ARE WOMEN GOING TO PREVENT OSTEO-POROSIS?

Ah, the final scare resorted to by the dairy people who are reeling so badly from the fat-and-cholesterol issue. Osteoporosis does *not* come from a low calcium intake. Bantu women consume less than one fourth of the amount of calcium recommended for American women, yet they nurse babies and are virtually free of osteoporosis—Mc-Dougall, pages 102, 52. So, after all the work you went through in our little quiz, it turns out you don't even need to eat much collards!

Preventing Osteoporosis

There are two simple steps to preventing osteoporosis (i.e. thin, porous bones):

1. Quit eating so much protein! (Yes, we're back to that again. Amazing how it all ties together, isn't it?) *The more protein you eat, the more calcium you need. The less protein you eat, the less calcium you need.* Since Americans routinely eat many times as much protein as they require (largely from all those dairy products they're consuming in an effort to get enough calcium!), many do have an artificial, protein-induced calcium deficiency in their bodies—McDougall, pages 100-102; Pritikin, pages 55, 390. The reason, if you're curious and don't want to look it up,

is that your body uses calcium to neutralize the ammonia and other toxic byproducts of metabolizing protein. Less protein, less calcium needed.

2. Exercise! There is a principle in nature known as "use it or lose it." Your body's survival instinct always wants it to hoard resources (food, energy, etc.) against any possible future shortage or famine, and therefore it will not expend those precious resources where they do not seem to be needed. Therefore anything which is not used regularly, be it your intellect, your sexual organs, or your bones, tends to rust, decay, or wither. Astronauts in space, despite calcium-rich American diets, experienced osteoporosis (bone loss) from their zero-gravity environment, which placed no weight-bearing demands upon their bones, until they started to carry rubber-band-type exercise equipment into space with them, to make their muscles and the bones to which they were attached perform difficult work. Take up some sport which will convince your body that strong bones are necessary—walking, running, aerobic dancing, weightlifting, cross-country skiing, whatever—and, if you haven't washed out all your calcium with excess protein, your body will believe you and provide them.—McDougall, page 177.

As a final point, what about the substantial number of our world today which still do not have domesticated dairy animals? And can you name another species, besides man, which drinks the milk of a different species—or drinks *any* milk, for that matter, after being weaned?

The answer, of course, is that all men and animals do just fine on the calcium found in their natural diets. And so will you.

OK, I'M CONVINCED. BUT SINCE YOU BROUGHT UP THE SUBJECT OF WOMEN, I'VE GOT ONE LAST QUESTION. YOU KNOW—IRON.

Yes, I know. And you know what to do. Take out a pencil and paper and number from one to three.

I'M SORRY I ASKED.

Too late. Question one: Which has more iron, eight ounces of T-bone steak (not counting the bone, of course!) or eight ounces of cooked black beans?

BY NOW I SHOULD FIGURE THE BLACK BEANS.

Right—6 milligrams of iron to 5.

BUT YOU SAID YOU ONLY EAT BEANS ONCE A WEEK OR SO. BESIDES, I KNOW THEY'RE HIGH IN PROTEIN, SO I SHOULDN'T EAT THEM TOO OFTEN, EITHER, SHOULD I?

Right on both counts! So let's take a look at millet, a nice, low-protein grain which you can eat every day if you like. (If you were not familiar with millet, you learned more about it in the chapter on Mexican cooking.) Question two: Which has more iron, a 400-calorie serving of the steak or a 400-calorie serving of millet?

I KNOW HOW TO PLAY THIS GAME. THE MILLET, BECAUSE THE STEAK HAS A LOT OF FAT AND SO IT TAKES A LOT LESS STEAK TO MAKE 400 CALORIES THAN IT DOES MILLET, RIGHT?

Very good—you learn quickly! The low-fat millet has 8 milligrams of iron, the fatty steak, 2 milligrams. But let's try it on an equal-weight basis. Third and final question: Which has more iron, eight ounces of millet or the eight-ounce steak?

FRANKLY, BY NOW I'M REALLY NOT SURE.

And you're quite right not to be. It comes out to a tie, at about 5 milligrams each. But let's look at the "cost" of those 5 milligrams of iron—what you get along with it in each food:

	Calories	Fat	Cholesterol
8 oz. steak	901	84g(!)	159mg
8 oz. millet	249	2g	0mg

Think about *that* the next time someone tells you that meat is the "best" source of iron. Best—by what standard?

By the way, please don't ever make the mistake of eating liver, in a misguided attempt to get iron or anything else. Yes, it's rich in iron, but it has over four times as much cholesterol as steak. Besides, think of the function of your liver. It not only filters and breaks down the alcohol you might be foolish enough to drink, but any other toxins or poisons in your bloodstream as well. Do you want to eat the part of the cow that filtered out all the cow's toxins?

CERTAINLY NOT! BUT ONE LAST QUESTION BEFORE I HEAD BACK TO THE GYM. CAN I REALLY GET STRONG WITHOUT MEAT, EGGS, AND DAIRY PRODUCTS?

I *could* give you dry, theoretical arguments to assure you that you can—Pritikin, pages 53-55. But instead I'll give you a real, live example, and a blonde to boot—my friend and helpmate Ruth. In May of 1985, after following essentially the dietary lifestyle described here for almost a year, Ruth won fourth place in her division at the Women's National Powerlifting Championships held in Chicago, where strict testing assures that contestants do not use steroids or other so-called "body-building" drugs. Ruth, who weighed in at 110 pounds, bench-pressed 120 pounds, did a squat (deep knee bend) with 215 pounds, and deadlifted (from floor to thighs) 285 pounds! Even our male readers would be hard pressed to do that. And how much more than 110 pounds would most men weigh?

285 POUNDS? UGH! I DON'T EVEN WANT TO THINK ABOUT IT! IT CERTAINLY SOUNDS AS THOUGH SHE GOT ENOUGH PROTEIN, IRON, AND CALCIUM, THOUGH—AND EVERYTHING ELSE FOR THAT MATTER. THE THOUGHT OF ALL THAT EXERCISE MAKES ME HUNGRY. WHEN DO WE EAT?

Glad you asked. We've just covered a whole world full of healthful vegetarian recipes. Now's the time to get started. The food tastes great!